Linford Christie

An Autobiography

Linford Christie
with Tony Ward

Stanley Paul
London Sydney Auckland Johannesburg

Thanks to Ron Roddan, Wendy Hoyte, Les Hoyte, the two physiotherapists Kerry and Dai, Terry Moule and all at West London without whom all this running would not have been possible.

Stanley Paul and Co. Ltd

An imprint of Century Hutchinson

Brookmount House, 62–65 Chandos Place, Covent Garden, London WC2N 4NW

Century Hutchinson Australia (Pty) Ltd 20 Alfred Street, Milsons Point, Sydney 2061, Australia

Century Hutchinson New Zealand Limited 191 Archers Road, PO Box 40–086, Glenfield, Auckland 10

Century Hutchinson South Africa (Pty) Ltd PO Box 337, Bergvlei 2012, South Africa

First printed 1989

Copyright © Linford Christie 1989

Set in Plantin by Selectmove Ltd

Printed and bound in Great Britain by MacKays of Chatham plc

ISBN 0 09 174179 3

The author and publishers wish to thank the following for permission to reproduce photographs:

In colour – AllSport, Associated Sports Photography, Colorsport, John Evans, Mark Shearman, Sport and General, Sporting Pictures (UK).

In black and white – Action-Plus Photographic, AllSport, Associated Sports Photography, Colorsport, *Fulham Chronicle*, Popperfoto, Rex Features, Mark Shearman, Frank Spooner, Times Newspapers.

In memory of
Gran–Anita Morrison

Contents

Introduction

When James and Mabel Christie came to Britain from Jamaica in the early 1960s they little knew that when their skinny young seven-year-old joined them, an embryonic sporting hero had arrived in the tradition of that island's great track athletes, mostly sprinters, who have graced the Olympic stadiums for the past forty years or more: Arthur Wint, George Rhoden, Herb McKenley, Don Quarrie, Grace Jackson, Ray Stewart, Merlene Ottey-Page for their native Jamaica; Ben Johnson, Atlee Mahorn, Milt Ottey, Charmaine Crooks, Angela Issajenko for Canada; Tessa Sanderson, Judy Simpson and now Linford Christie for Great Britain.

This is Linford's story, from his very early days in Kingston to the exciting and also traumatic events of the 1988 Olympic Games in Seoul. In sprinting terms he is one of the greatest – the fastest ever European, the only athlete to beat even-time for the 100 metres, and one of only five men in history to achieve that feat at sea-level. His is an enormous talent that has come slowly to the boil, although not through any innate drive, for in his early years he epitomized the stereotype West Indian youth – happy-go-lucky, easy-come easy-go, relying almost solely on his great natural ability. The signals were often there that if he would only commit himself to his talent he could achieve greater things, but always he chose to ignore them. However, when finally that realization came and he made the commitment, it was total. Almost immediately, as if a fairy queen had waved a magic wand, he fulfilled his promise in some of the great stadiums of the world.

There is a history of sprinting in Linford's family, but from whom did he inherit the doggedness to succeed, the discipline that he finally displayed to reach the top of his profession – for we must call it that because, as he himself says, 'Sprinting is my business'? Certainly much of it came from a very great woman, the inspiration of the whole family:

his grandmother Anita Morrison, who had a enormous influence on his life, especially during his formative years. He frequently reveals his love for her, and indeed his whole family, as his story unfolds.

This is very human story. The Jamaicans and other West Indians who emigrated in the fifties and sixties were the great pioneers of their age. They left their roots and families and crossed the seas to what they thought of as the Promised Land. What must have been their impression on arrival is anybody's guess. Fathers and mothers left children four thousand miles away to come to Britain, often to scrimp and toil at the most menial jobs in order that the rest of the family could follow. The grandmothers, the great matriarchs, shouldered the family burden in their absence. It was the norm, and the Christies were no different from anybody else.

Linford and I talked for almost fifteen hours in preparation for this book. As he told his story an extraordinary honesty shone through. He did not shirk from examining critically some of his less than glorious moments. Nor did he shirk from making forthright comment about the behaviour of others as it affected him! He has a simple, straightforward approach to life which is refreshing. Deviousness is not a concept he understands. Warmth and love are essential parts of his nature, and it is to these that the public so enthusiastically respond.

As with many stories of black men and women living in Britain, the spectre of racism is often unavoidable. That this is a canker on our society there can be no doubt. As Linford unfolded the details of how he and his family have been harassed and racially abused, he became very emotional indeed, the painful memories rekindling in him the utter frustration and impotent anger that he, his father, his whole family have felt and still feel. It is, sadly, a story that could be repeated thousands of times in Britain, and it is hardly surprising that many in the black community will say: 'If it can happen to Linford Christie, then what chance do we stand?'

Many have recovered from this injustice, and some have forgiven, but as I watched Linford taking a lap of honour at the indoor track at Cosford after winning the 200 metres title there in January this year – the applause overwhelming, the crowd standing, eager to take his hand, the reciprocal affection very evident – I could not help but feel that double standards were being applied somewhere, that perhaps some Britons wanted it both ways. If this book goes just a small way to righting that wrong, then both of us will have succeeded.

Tony Ward
May, 1989

1
Showdown in Seoul

As dawn broke over the South Korean capital of Seoul, the sky turned from the black of night to the light azure of early morning, promising another hot day. In the Olympic Village, built south of the Han River, there was as yet little life stirring inside the concrete apartments. Flags of various nations hung from balconies. The ubiquitous sentries, rifles slung over their shoulders, stretched and yawned. Occasionally long-distance runners would jog past, chatting quietly, their daily devotions almost done.

It was the second day of athletics events of the Games of the XXIVth Olympiad. Already one running champion had been crowned, the diminutive Portuguese Rosa Mota, winner of the women's marathon in just under two and a half hours. On this day we would come to the other end of the running spectrum, to the fastest men and women on earth whose triumphs would depend upon mere hundredths of a second in the 100 metres. In two rounds of sprinting heats on the previous day, the wheat had been sorted from the chaff. The fastest man had been the American Carl Lewis, with 9.99 seconds; the slowest was Samuel Birch of Liberia, with 11.68. Thirty-four of the women sprinters had run faster than this, but there was none to match Florence Griffith-Joyner, the Californian world-record holder, the incomparable 'Flo-Jo' destined to take the gold medal.

Sixteen men were left in the 100 metres, already sorted by computer into two semi-finals; eight would progress to the final. Two of the favourites were asleep away from the Village, in downtown Seoul. Ben Johnson, the world champion and record holder from Canada, was at the Hilton Hotel; Lewis, the defending champion here, was at a secret address in a specially rented house with his family. Two others were in their team headquarters: the American Calvin Smith, the former world-record holder, and the British favourite Linford

Christie, sharing a room on the top floor of the team's apartment with his friend, the hurdler Colin Jackson.

I awoke early – too early – but there was no going back to sleep. The light poured in through the window of our room. I felt comfortable and relaxed, much better than the previous day when I hadn't slept at all, worried about whether my injury would stand up, whether I had come all this way for nothing. It had stood up, of course, and I had the confidence of the first two rounds now, of having the second fastest time behind Carl and of beating Ben. I had gone to bed about midnight. I believe in going to bed when you are really tired, not when you think you should. Then you usually lie there just staring at the ceiling, thinking about everything that could go wrong.

I got up and dressed quickly and as quietly as I could, but Colin was awake and he mumbled a 'good luck' as I headed for the door. I managed some breakfast, met up with Colin's coach Malcolm Arnold who was taking me down to the track, and we walked in the sunshine to where the buses waited to run the shuttle to the Olympic Stadium. I was still feeling pretty good within myself.

At the warm-up track, which was alongside the stadium, I had my usual massage and began my leisurely warm-up. I could see some of the other sprinters jogging around – Carl, Ben, Ray, Calvin – and gave one or two a wave. I went to the first Reporting Area in good time. Here the officials checked your number and gave you your side number, for the photo finish. Then we walked through to another room, under the stand, where they checked us again, politely but methodically. After about five minutes we went into the final check room where we stayed for what seemed ages, most of us in our pre-race trances now, nobody speaking, just moving about, staying loose. Occasionally I glanced at the TV screen that was showing events already taking place.

Then we went outside, into the stadium, through a last security gate, into the bright morning sunshine. The adrenalin was pumping but I knew that I could control it, knew that it was necessary to a good performance. I even had the audacity to think that I was going to win. I thought that Ben hadn't had anything left when I had beaten him in the second round the previous day. They kept us hanging around for a while. My mind was a blank; I automatically went through some drills and some stretching. Then they called us to our marks.

Ben got away to a really fast start and there was no heading him. About ten metres from the finish I knew that I had qualified and eased, finishing second ahead of Dennis Mitchell. I felt elated at beating Dennis, he was rated a medal hope. I saw from the clock that Ben had run 10.03, not as fast as Carl, who had gone below ten seconds again. I watched the re-run of the race on the big stadium scoreboard, checked that I had run second and then went back under to collect my kit from the airless, sweat-filled room where it had been taken from the start. I was in my first Olympic final.

All the world wanted to see this race. About half a billion people in total were gathered around television sets. The pre-race hype had been worthy of any world heavyweight boxing match, on a par with Ali and Frazier. In Britain, as a grey day dawned, half a million peered, red-eyed, at their screens. In Australia, in Melbourne Park, a hundred thousand people sat waiting for the Victorian Football League Cup Final, and while they waited the 100 metres was to be relayed on the stadium scoreboard from Seoul.

Past champions also watched, wondering if history would be made on this day. No man had won the Olympic 100 metres twice in the modern celebrations of the Games. Now Carl Lewis, the champion from Los Angeles, had that chance. The 1980 winner, Allan Wells, sat in a television studio in London; in Dallas, Texas, the man rated by some as the fastest of them all, Bob Hayes, the 1964 champion from Tokyo, sat watching and waiting, memories stirring in him; and Harrison Dillard watched from Cleveland, Ohio, the oldest living sprint gold medallist, winner at London's Wembley Stadium in 1948. In the stands in Seoul was the Russian Valeriy Borzov, winner in Munich in 1972.

The stadium was packed beyond capacity; in every nook and cranny people crammed together, standing four deep on the walkways and filling the steps between the seats. Coaches and managers of the finalists were now gripped with the tension of the approaching moment of truth, like expectant fathers at the birth, now impotent, their work done. And that tension spread to every tier of every stand as the eight finalists – three Americans, two Canadians and one each from Jamaica, Brazil and Britain – came into the stadium.

We had a one-and-a-half-hour wait between semi and final. Joan Watt, our physiotherapist, gave me a massage. She is a lovely lady as well as a great physio, and we chatted away as she worked on my legs. I sat around for a while, talking to people. I didn't feel at all tense and I suppose that I have to thank Carl a little bit for that.

Some weeks beforehand, I think perhaps when we were in Japan, I had read an article that Carl had written in which he said that in the Zurich race in August, when he had trounced Ben, he had not deliberately tried to race anybody but had gone out on to the track to run his own race, do his own thing. He said that all he had done was run how he knew best and that he had kept totally relaxed by not bothering about anybody else. I thought about this and came to the conclusion that it seemed a very good philosophy. In most competitions I was tense; I was racing, I was aware of the opposition and what they were doing. I went out there and ran on their terms. I wanted to beat them; I tried too hard. I thought that Carl could be right about this – better to get out, relax and concentrate on what I was doing and not on anybody else.

When the draw was announced and I found that I was next to Carl Lewis I thought that it was just brilliant, because we run our races in a similar fashion and I thought he could drag me through. If I had been super-lucky and they had put Carl next to Ben as well as next to me, then I think I might have beaten Carl – but of course, that is entirely hypothetical!

I had another massage, warmed up again, tuned into my Walkman and then went through the reporting procedures for the fourth time in two days. Then we walked out into the stadium. You could feel the excitement, hear the buzz of antici-pation. And why not? The 100 metres is the classic; everybody wants to be the fastest man in the world. I saw lots of British people all over the stadium, waving huge Union Jacks. It really made me feel good. There were cries of 'Come on, Linford!' and 'Go, Linford!' Even people who weren't British were calling out my name. I suppose that many people went there to support a particular person. It really makes you feel fantastic that people from all walks of life come out to support you. It makes you want to do that much better.

The starter called us to our marks. I just looked straight down the track, set my tunnel vision and climbed into my blocks. The gun fired, and we were away. I was really close to Carl. I could see him out of the corner of my eye and I thought, I'm going to stick with him. It flashed through my mind that I was close. I thought, try a little harder, go faster. I closed the gap, but he had gained at the start and that is what gave him the advantage at the finish.

It was over, and we eased down. Now we could hear the noise. I thought for a moment that I had come second; I hadn't seen Ben at all. Then I watched the re-run on the screen and saw that I had come third. I looked at the time and saw that it was a new world record, so I thought that I, too, must have run fast. I felt marvellous and punched the air. Then I got my time and felt even better – the time was more important to me than the medal. Europe has been around for a few thousand years and to be the first European under ten seconds . . . well! I think that the record will remain for a long, long time.

I felt the happiest I think I have ever felt. My first Olympic final; the bronze medal; European record of 9.97 seconds. Now I was up with the world's elite sprinters, with Ben and Carl, Calvin and Dennis. A lot of people had doubted me, had said that I wouldn't get anywhere. Now here I was in the greatest race of all time, with four men under ten seconds.

A few years ago – before 1986 – I was at a party with a few friends and we met some people who used to be in athletics. They said, 'So you're still at it, then; isn't it about time you packed it in?' I told them I was going to be the British number one. A girl among them said, 'You must be joking. I've heard all this before.' This and similar instances stayed in my mind, because I believe that I am a competitor in every sense of the word, always ready to take up a challenge. I wanted to show those people who had mocked and doubted. Standing around at the finish, I remembered all of them.

I talked to Kevin Cosgrove for the BBC and to Mori Plant for Australian television. There was high excitement; the race had lived up to all expectations. Ben had surprised them all again. I went across to talk to Jim Rosenthal for ITV. 'You said all year, Linford,' Jim said, 'that you were going to produce it here in Seoul. One or two people said that you weren't in the Americans' league.'

'*Track and Field News* said that I wouldn't do anything,' I replied. 'Last year they were right. This year, absolutely wrong.'

I drifted away down the steps and collected my gear. It doesn't hit you for a long time what you have achieved. You simply get taken along by the system, people crowding around you, the press anxious for interviews. We went to Doping Control, where pieces of paper for me to sign were pushed under my nose and there was a lot of shouting in Korean. It was chaotic; people were over-excited and anxious. The system had cracked.

We walked out for the victory ceremony and stood behind the plinth. From where I was standing I could see all the British athletes and supporters, cheering and celebrating. I could see Myrtle Augee, Mary Berkeley and Tessa Sanderson, all waving and shouting, seeming to make more noise than the rest of the stadium. Then the American announcer said, 'The bronze medal, Linford Christie, Great Britain,' and I was up on the plinth, the medal was around my neck and the Union Jacks were waving. In a word, it was great. They played the Canadian anthem and we waved our flowers at the crowd.

Afterwards, I gave my sample at Doping Control without too much trouble. Sometimes it is awkward because with all the excitement you tend to go to the lavatory a number of times before the race, which leads to difficulty later on. I then went to an ITV studio to talk by satellite to my coach Ron Roddan in London. He had gone back to Britain after leaving the holding camp in Japan.

'What did you think of the race?' I asked him. I was anxious to know.

'I think it's the best race you've even run,' he replied.

I wanted to find out if there had been any mistakes, so I asked Ron if he had spotted any. If he hadn't, then I would have to retire! 'You tied up a little bit towards the end,' said Ron, and that made me feel good. It meant there was more to come.

Out on the warm-up track, around the tent that the medical staff had set up as our headquarters, everyone crowded round and there were handshakes and smiles. Everybody was happy, especially about the time. Back in London in Shepherds Bush the celebrations would, I knew, be under way, led by my Dad, my greatest supporter. When the excitement had died down I thought about my family, of all their help and sacrifices over the years and of the hardships they had undergone to bring us all up. And on this, one of the very best days of my life, I thought about my grandmother and how she had loved and cared for me when I was very young in Jamaica. My one sadness was that she had died too early to witness my successes.

2
Island in the Sun

They call Jamaica the 'Island in the Sun', and that is my memory of it. Of sunshine, warmth and abundant fruit growing every-where, and of love. I was born on 2 April 1960 in St Andrews in Kingston. There were two sisters ahead of me in the family, and though of course I did not know it, there was heady talk of emigration, possibly to Canada but more usually to England, the land of milk and honey and opportunity. I guess that plans were already being made when I was born, for a year or so later my Dad left for London. Two years after that, when he had saved enough money, my Mum went as well and I was left in the care of my grandmother, Anita Morrison. I stayed with her, in her house near the centre of Kingston, until I was seven years old. My grandmother therefore moulded my life, and I believe I am all the better for it.

This was all fairly normal. Emigrating to better yourself was a dream for most Jamaicans, a dream many were determined to fulfil. Families were close – there was no shunting the old people aside as can happen in Northern Europe. Grandmothers were an integral part of life and so, when the mass emigrations began, it seemed perfectly right and natural for them to take over the running of the families left behind. After all, they had the experience.

We were a large family. There was my elder half-brother Trevor and my two older sisters Lisa and Lorraine and me, and there were also three cousins who were left in the same way. The houses were big and detached, and there was enough room in most back yards to build another two or three. At the front of my grandmother's house one of my older cousins ran a shop. My earliest memories were of the fruit trees. I cannot remember ever feeling hungry; you didn't have to go looking for food, you just picked it off the trees.

My grandmother was an imposing woman, five feet nine or ten inches tall. Running such a large family didn't present any problems for her. I'm sure she enjoyed it and that it gave her a purpose in life. As far as I know there was never any shortage of money – our fathers sent sums regularly back from England – and I, being the youngest, was the centre of attention. In many ways those were the happiest days of my life.

Grandmothers can be contrary people. They are often strict, but they usually also spoil you. At least, that is the way it was with mine and I don't believe there has ever been a nicer person. She ran the family like a military operation: each of us, no matter how young, had our tasks. I remember that we didn't have a tap in the house but used a communal tap from which we had to fill two barrels in our garden. Every morning before we went to school, we all had to take a bucket appropriate to our size and run a relay from the communal tap to the barrels until they were full. In the beginning, when I was two or three, I couldn't reach the barrel – but I still had to join in. My sisters had to sweep the yard before they went to school. My grandmother would give orders to the eldest and these would be passed down – as I got older I found this particularly galling! But I can tell you, no one shirked and discipline was strict.

There never was a greater story-teller than my granny. She had an abundance of tales from the old colonial days, when she had been cook for a white family. She was born before the turn of the century, so it is likely that her parents had been born into slavery. My grandfather had died early, so she was used to bringing up a family on her own. I guess that it gave her a sense of independence and allowed her personality, which was fairly dominant, to develop.

At the age of three or four I went to a nursery school which was about three or four doors away from our house. Education for Jamaicans was a top priority; people at home would take time out to teach us. At nursery I knew my times-tables to twelve, and could read. A couple of years later I went to primary school and came under the strict, disciplined regime that was usual in Jamaica in those days. Learning was by rote and strictly formal, and we practised copy-book writing. Every morning we were read a verse from the Bible and had to remember it by heart.

The teacher would call us up to the front of the class to recite it, and woe betide anyone who faltered.

School uniform was always worn, which for the boys meant khaki shirts and trousers. At 8.55 a.m., school checking-in time, the teacher at the gate would check your fingernails and your ears, and would take a pencil and pull it through your hair – if the pencil got stuck then you would be sent home to tidy up. Then, when you returned, school would have started and they would beat you for being late. All school books had to be covered in brown paper, and you were in trouble if they became dog-eared. If they gave you ten sums, you were allowed to get only one wrong. More than that and you would get a belt on your hand for every one that was incorrect. Often you would get beaten twice, once at school and then again when you arrived back home, for getting into trouble! To answer questions you stood up, and you always called the teacher 'Sir' or 'Miss'. When I answered my grandmother I always said 'Yes, Granny', or 'No, Granny'.

This, then, was the Jamaican norm, and when I came to Britain, which was still in the throes of the 'Swinging Sixties', I found the comparative indiscipline in schools difficult to cope with. In Jamaica, you could not avoid learning. I imagine that many older people in Britain will recognize this type of education, and I suppose it was a legacy passed on to us by our former colonial overlords. I believe that it was a good inheritance, and one that has stood me in good stead all my life.

My Dad came over from England to see how we were getting on. I hadn't known him when he had left for Britain, but when I saw him I somehow knew that he was my father. He talked to us about the new country, about snow, about the huge city, and we all wanted to know more, to see what it was like. He also told me that I now had a younger brother, Russell, which made me feel excited and wonder that he could be like. I didn't know it at the time, but he had come to prepare us for the move to England. Six months later my grandmother told me that I was going to join my parents and that she, too, was emigrating. It was the end of my time in the Caribbean, of the sheltered, warm, family life that I had known there, and the beginning of a new and exciting era.

We flew to Heathrow by British Overseas Airways Corporation, as it was then. Sitting next to me on the plane was a Mrs Jackson.

For almost the whole flight I kept asking her about life in England. She had been there before and was very tolerant of the young man plying her with questions. At last year's AAA Championships she turned up, found me and introduced herself. She had seen me on television and remembered the skinny little boy, Linford Christie, who had asked her all those questions on a flight from Kingston twenty-one years earlier. It felt really good to see her again, and I was touched that, after all these years, she had remembered me.

It was September when we flew in, so there wasn't all that dramatic a change in temperature – that was still to come! My Dad met us at the airport and, of course, the first thing that I wanted to do was to see my younger brother Russell. Russell was then five. We lived in Shepherds Bush in Loftus Road, in the shadow of Queen's Park Rangers' ground and also close to the great White City Stadium. My parents were tenants and the house was very basic – the sink was outside and the cooker was on the landing. We arrived at the house and my Dad introduced me to a woman.

'This is your Mum,' he said. I thought, 'No, my granny is my Mum.'

Of course I called her Mum, but it took me quite a little while to accept her as my mother. I had, naturally heard all about her, but deep, deep down inside I missed my granny. Even though I knew she would soon be in England, I also knew that she wasn't going to live with us but with my cousins in Nottingham, and I guess I was sad about that. My Mum and I are now the very best of friends, not really like mother and son. The more I grew up, the more I got to like her. It must have been awful to be separated from her children, as she and many other Jamaican mothers were. I suppose that because she hadn't really known me from an early age, she made a tremendous effort to get to know me later. So we became good friends.

England was strange and disappointing. There was no gold on the pavements, as the myths in Jamaica had foretold. Back home it had always been warm. Everyone was friendly and said 'Hello' when you passed by on the street; in Kingston you knew everybody and they knew you. Here, it wasn't like that. The roads were busy, the buildings were grey and drab; there were tall, high-rise blocks. It was totally unlike Jamaica, the houses all small and packed close together. In my grandmother's house

I had had a big bedroom; here I had to share. At that age it was a great disillusionment.

Worse was to come, because there followed a very cold winter, and I had never felt cold in my life before. Then came the biggest shock: snow. White flakes came out of the sky and Dad smiled, pointed and said, 'That's snow!' I rushed outside, looked up and opened my mouth to let the flakes drop in. The snow settled on my tongue and it was so cold that I cried. My toes went numb, and at the primary school that we attended I wasn't allowed to wear long trousers at my age. The teachers made us go out to play in the snowbound playground and I joined in with all the fun, sliding around in the snow and slush, throwing snowballs, all the usual things. Suddenly, as my shoes and socks got soaking wet and frozen, there came an excruciating pain and I cried with the intensity of it. I didn't know what was happening to me!

It was also at Canberra Primary School in White City that I first realized that I was black. In Jamaica I had never seen a white person; to us youngsters they were an unknown quantity. At Canberra the ratio of black children to white was about even, so there was no way that I felt out of place or different. There were the usual games in the playground, children chasing each other, boys grabbing girls, everybody laughing and enjoying themselves. I joined in, and I ran after a little white girl and grabbed her. She turned to me and said, 'You can't play. My Mummy said I mustn't play with blackies.'

I stopped dead. 'Ay, I'm black!' flashed through my mind. I looked at my hands and legs. 'I'm black!' Up until that moment I had seen myself as simply a person; colour of skin hadn't registered with me. No one had ever called me a little 'blackie' in Kingston, because we were all the same.

What had happened didn't really sink home for another two years or so. Then suddenly, every morning when I arrived at school two kids would stand by the gate and shout out, 'Nigger, nigger, pull your trigger! Bang, bang, bang!' It hurt. I told Mum that kids at school were calling me 'Nigger'. She said, 'If they are calling you "Nigger", call them "White Honkey"!' This sort of exchange went on for a long time. It was spiteful and hurtful to me. At Canberra, gangs would try to beat me up; in Jamaica there were fights, but they were one to one. In England even the playground football matches were black versus white, so I gradually became conscious of the distinction, aware of colour. It was all something of an embittering experience.

Finally, one day a boy called Charlie bawled out, 'Nigger!' at me and I chased him in a fury. I'd had enough; I couldn't take it any more. I wanted to fight back. My Mum and Dad let me discover all this for myself. They would never have dreamed of telling me to take a certain attitude towards white people. I was always brought up to treat everybody as I find them.

I also found the standards of education at Canberra behind those of Jamaica. The formal methods of teaching, the accent on the 'three Rs', had stood me in good stead and in those aspects of school work I was ahead. I felt when I came here that I was going backwards. The discipline that I had experienced in my schools in Kingston was just not there.

So life went on and I adapted to my new country, to living as a black youngster in a white-dominated society. Life at home was good, I had become used to living with my parents, and gradually I integrated at school. One day, a year or so after I had landed at Heathrow, I was playing football in the playground, chasing the ball over the yard in the way of primary school kids, when a teacher, Mr Wright came up to me. 'You look pretty nippy,' he said. 'Would you like to run for the school?' It was the beginning of my long road to the Olympic Games in Seoul.

3
Running Raw

My very first race was at the White City Stadium. I'm actually quite proud of that. The old stadium was in its penultimate year as an athletics venue. It was 1968 and the Crystal Palace track had been converted to Tartan in readiness for the Mexico City Olympic Games which were to be held on synthetic surfacing for the first time. However, at the tender age of eight I was unaware of all this as I marched from the back gate of Canberra, across a narrow road and into White City for the Borough Primary School Sports. We had had our school trial in the concrete playground and I had made the team; so here I was, complete with black Curtis plimsolls (I had had to ask my Mum to buy me a pair) and white 'Alf Ramsey' shorts.

A young man called Fitzroy Stanislav, from Victoria School, was taking part. He asked me, 'How are you going to run this race?'

'I'm going to start slowly and build up,' I replied. The race was all of 80 metres! I can't remember where I finished.

Life moved on. My Dad bought his own house in Shepherds Bush, for about £5500. My cousins had tried to persuade him to move to Nottingham where housing was much cheaper, but he liked London and stuck it out until he could afford to buy. He had worked tremendously hard since his arrival in Britain, first to bring over his family and then to buy his own house. The family grew still larger with the birth of my sister Anita. We are seven in number altogether, with me right in the middle.

The house move necessitated my moving school, to Brackenbury in Hammersmith where I began in the third year. There were no school sports and no athletics, just football, and that is what I played for the rest of the time I was there. I have to say that I was no budding Garth Crooks or John Fashanu, but I was fairly useful and could score goals.

When I was eleven I moved to secondary school, Henry Compton in Fulham. They gave us a list of the clothes and equipment we would need, and Dad bought me a pair of spikes from Ron Springett's Sports Shop. I remember them well; they were blue leather and had four spikes and I was the proudest youngster alive in possessing them. I took them to school for Sports Day and decided to try them out by sprinting across the school gymnasium, and I spiked up the wooden floor rather badly. It was not an auspicious start to my time there and the physical education staff were, to say the least, not well pleased!

Henry Compton was a good school, and I was a reasonable pupil – no cherub, but no devil either. The mix of black and white was, as at Canberra, about even, but there was no racial tension. I experienced far more racism at primary school than I ever did at secondary, which was perhaps unusual.

I ran for the school from the first year onwards, and this helped me tremendously. It takes you out of the ruck and you find that you obtain some respect. If you discover that you are talented at something, it helps you to relax. The school was very keen on athletics and had a tradition in the sport. We were encouraged by our PE teachers, of which there were two Mr Joneses and a Mr Davies – by whose names you might guess that the school was also good at rugby! We used to have House matches at the Hurlingham track, and I remember one afternoon competing in the 100, 200 and 400 metres and the three jumps – high, long and triple. I used to dread these latter events, especially the high jump because we used to land in unraked sand! We also took part in the Hammersmith Schools Sports event at the West London Stadium. I ran for the school up to and including the third year and then I stopped, though I can't remember why, although I was fourteen, which is, as most young men will tell you, a funny age.

I was not the best around. There was Grant Ward, who was not only the fastest boy in the school but, so it was reputed, at one time, in all of London as well. We used to have student teachers in from what was then called Borough Road Training College. It had a big name in athletics and some of our boys went on to be students there, so the reputation of Henry Compton was high in the field of sport.

I resumed running in my fifth year at the school, winning the

200 metres in the school sports and coming second in the 100 and 400 metres. Nobody knew how to run the longer events, the advice we were given being the same as that I had pontificated for 80 metres back at the White City: start slowly and build up! I ran the 100 metres at the Hammersmith Schools Sports and came second, being beaten by my schoolmate Victor Ajai. He was picked to run in the London Schools at Crystal Palace but withdrew, so I had my first opportunity to run outside the immediate neighbourhood of school and borough, in a new environment on an international track.

Your first London Schools event in those days was quite an experience. There were literally thousands of competitors from all the London boroughs, along with an equal number of supporters and spectators. The noise was bedlam and the predominant skin colour was black, for reaching the secondary schools now were the offspring of the wave of immigrants of the late fifties and early sixties. The fastest in my age group, however, was a white boy called Stapleton who went on to beat Mike McFarlane at the English Schools event. The meeting has deteriorated sharply in recent years, in both standard and numbers taking part, and that is a great tragedy.

I left Henry Compton after my fifth year and went to Wandsworth Technical College to study electronics (which was the 'in' thing in those days), as I was interested in amplifying and building electrical equipment. I was also working for Visionhire and hating every minute of it. It was supposed to be work experience, but I didn't do much work other than stare at the test card, and this was a pretty boring experience. I decided that it was not for me and moved over to accountancy – I had always been reasonable at maths – working for the Co-op and attending college part time. This enabled me still to compete in the Hammersmith and London Schools. At the Hammersmith Schools at West London Stadium, the ground was always packed and there was a lot of enthusiasm and a good deal of betting on the races going on. Everyone came along there simply to enjoy it.

Mr Jones, my old PE teacher, had advised me to join an athletics club, so I went to West London Stadium, not far up from the old White City and adjacent to Wormwood Scrubs Prison. I turned up there in jeans and a jumper, but with a new pair of spikes. I had progressed to Golas, which were quite well known in the seventies. There were two snags to the shoes: one was that there was no cushioning whatsoever for your feet, and the other was the dye. My pair were purple and black, so that when it rained they dyed my socks, which did not impress my mother at all. I wrote on my spikes: Sonia Lannaman – Speed Queen! Sonia was one of the first of the black running stars and had run at all the major meetings and been on television. She was the first athlete that I could identify myself with; she was always in the news. I wanted to be like Sonia Lannaman.

When I arrived, a little nervously, at West London, I was introduced to a man called Ron Roddan, a sprint coach who trained people such as Trevor Hoyte and Steve Green, both internationals. Ron doesn't remember this tall, slightly gawky figure approaching him at all. He told me just to run around and do some starts, which is the way I guess most athletes begin when they join a club. His club was Thames Valley Harriers, one of the country's top names in the British Athletics League, and both it and West London Stadium were bristling with internationals. I soon became bored, realizing that I wasn't going to get much chance to compete for the club – my best time was 23.3 seconds for 200 metres – so I joined the second club with its headquarters at the track, London Irish, which was more intimate and not quite so awe-inspiring. I know that the number of black athletes running for London Irish causes some amusement but the club is absolutely ideal for the young or up-and-coming athlete, and the people who run it deserve a lot of credit.

In 1979 I went to the English Schools Championships for the first time, to run in the 200 metres for London. The meeting was held in Harvey Haddon Stadium in Nottingham, and it was the first time that I had ever been on an Inter-City train. I stood by the door feeling very nervous. The train seemed to travel so quickly and when another Inter-City passed by going the other way, seemingly only inches away, I thought that here was Armageddon! I was scared out of my mind.

The English Schools was an entirely new experience. Competing there were the cream of the country's young athletic talent, some of them already making a name for themselves at international level. The meeting lasted two days and the competitors were billeted out in the homes of local schoolchildren. It was exciting with the march past of all the counties of England, everyone chanting slogans and supporting each other. In those days I was known as 'Horse' because it was said that I galloped, so the cries from team-mates Mike Powell and Ossie Cham were 'Come on, Horse!' 'Relax, Horse!' – which occasioned a few odd glances. My main opposition in the final was Phil Brown from Birmingham, already an established international and the man who over the next decade or so was to be a team-mate of mine and to be the British anchorman in some very fine 4 × 400 metres relay performances. We lined up in the final and I came off the bend well in the lead. Then came a new cry, which rather overshadowed my friends' efforts: 'West Mids – Best Kids!' chanted over and over by sixty or more voices. To me it was electric, like the Olympic Games. I was totally inexperienced, and on the straight I eased and Phil came past like the Inter-City train I had travelled on. He won in 21.5, and I ran 21.8 seconds. He came up to me afterwards. 'Who are you?' he asked.

'I'm Linford Christie,' I replied.

'Who's your coach?' asked Phil in a rather persistent manner. 'I've never heard of you.'

'I haven't got one,' I said.

'You'd better start training,' Phil said. 'You could be good!'

That year the British Amateur Athletic Board issued some questionnaires at the English Schools Championships asking athletes what they needed in order to help them improve. I sent mine back to John Le Masurier, a former National Coach and now in charge of the Team Secretariat, saying that I needed more competition. A few weeks later I received an invitation to compete at an international meeting in Gateshead, the Amoco Games.

It was my first taste of big-time athletics, and my first visit to Gateshead. It was the furthest north I had ever travelled and the first thing that struck me was the strangeness of the dialect. I had never heard anything like the Geordie accent before, and in the beginning it was unintelligible to me. The second thing I noticed was the friendliness of the people, the spontaneity of their welcome and their kindness to all the athletes who gathered there. Gateshead is now my favourite stadium; the crowd is highly knowledgeable and turns out to support us in all weathers.

The International Stadium was five years old when I first arrived. It was inspired by Brendan Foster and it brought international athletics to the town and put it on the map. I was running in the 100 and 200 metres with some very imposing names: Don Quarrie, who was the Olympic 200 metres champion from Montreal three years earlier; Allan Wells, the British number one; James Gilkes from Guyana, a world-class runner; and the big, imposing figure of Haseley Crawford, the Montreal 100 metres gold medallist.

It rained on the day – not unusual in Tyneside. Haseley Crawford was trying to intimidate everybody, which I later learned was his usual pre-race gambit. 'I'm smoking! I'm smoking!' he said urgently to the opposition. He was in my heat and we went down to the start to fix our blocks into the Tartan. My lane was clear; Haseley had water in his. I set up my blocks but Haseley took them up, put them in his lane and so changed with me. No words were exchanged; he just did it. Now Haseley was big, really big, and I was the smallest there, a raw recruit to the international scene. There was nothing I could do. I qualified for the B final. Using his brains, so did Don Quarrie. It was the end of a very interesting season.

I was beginning to think of myself as an athlete, though not a very serious one. I didn't care whether or not I lost. I had run in the trials for the European Junior Championships and finished fifth in the 100 metres in 10.6 seconds, wind assisted. I ran 21.6 seconds, again wind assisted, for the 200 metres and didn't make the team. The stars of my age group in those days were Mike Powell and Mike McFarlane. Mac, as everybody calls him, won the European Junior that year. I admire Mac because he has remained at the top of British sprinting for a decade through a lot of hard work. A lot of athletes have had more natural ability than he has, but Mac has persevered. His career has had its ups and downs. Each time it looked as though he was going to make his breakthrough – in 1982 after his Commonwealth dead heat with Allan Wells, or in 1984 after making the Los Angeles Olympic final, or again in 1985 after winning the European Indoor – he just didn't get his act together.

At club level I did a lot of long and triple jumping, making 14.25 metres at the latter. I was sprinting in all the B League races for London Irish, winning all the time and getting fed up with it; there was no real challenge. One of my friends in those days was Magary Effiong, a man with a great natural talent, at decathlon almost as great, I think, as Daley Thompson. He could come out and jump well over seven metres on no training at all. I thought that I could do the same in sprinting.

I was living at home and working well at the Co-op in Hammersmith, dealing with ledger sales, counting the cash, keeping it flowing. Then I was promoted to assistant cashier at the Wandsworth branch where I had to deal with the toll accounts to go to head office as well as the share accounts and the dividends. I quite enjoyed it. The only problem with the job was that I had to work on a lot of Saturdays, which naturally interfered with my athletics, though the company were quite generous in giving me time off. After a day's work and a trip to Wormwood Scrubs on a number 220 bus, arriving in the dark and perhaps the cold, I was not inclined to put in further effort. And I didn't.

I was now training under Ron Roddan, but still had a very casual approach. If Ron announced a long or tough session I simply would not do it. I would retire with one or two others to Mick's café adjacent to the track and play dominoes. Sometimes these domino sessions in the canteen would last from 6.30 p.m. until midnight. They also got very noisy, which must have been galling for Ron, standing out in the wind and rain supervising the keen members of his squad. At the time he didn't make any comment, though I'm sure he thought quite a lot!

My problem, if you can call it that, at the time was that I thought I had all the natural talent in the world and didn't need to train. I was really enjoying my running, but part of that enjoyment was in beating people who I knew trained hard, people like Phil Brown and Mike Powell. I got quite a few kicks out of doing that. The way I viewed training was that it got me out of the house.

I then joined the Air Training Corps, 336 Squadron, White City. A good friend of mine had joined and I really liked the uniform. I didn't, however, like the discipline, the constant marching, the drill, the saluting. It was too much like being in the Army – which, on reflection, was hardly surprising. But I ran for them and won most everything, so it was good fun, and it also kept me off the streets, which pleased my parents.

I was part of a typical black family. My parents were stricter with us than my granny had ever been. The traditional and most important essence of life was obtaining a good education, which to the black immigrants was the key to success, a way out of the ruck. Most parents dreamed of their offspring becoming lawyers, doctors, teachers – professions they thought that good schooling could provide. Many had also learnt from bitter experience that a good education was needed in the continuing battle against colour prejudice.

It was a perfectly natural point of view. My parents, like thousands of other black people, had scrimped and scraped and saved for years to ensure that we had a better life. The jobs they had when they came to Britain were menial, jobs that nobody else would deign to do. They did all that so that we would have better opportunities, and they expected us to grab them when they came along. They also expected us to obtain our education as quickly as possible and then go out to work straight away to take our share of supporting the family. Dad always said that he wanted me to seize all the opportunities that he had missed. I suppose that I shall say the same thing to my family when the time comes. Even over ten generations, the same story will be repeated.

Sport didn't have any priority at all in this kind of philosophy; with Mum and Dad it was way down low on the list. One day I came home from training and Mum asked, 'How much do they pay you for all this running?'

I laughed. 'You go just because you enjoy it,' I replied.

'You mean to say that you go out in all weathers – hail, rain, snow, sunshine – and run up and down for nothing?'

I said, 'That's how it goes, Mum.'

She was totally nonplussed.

On another occasion I came home with a pulled hamstring. I was very prone to them at the time, mainly because I was undertaking only light and sometimes very spasmodic training. Dad went berserk. He said that I was killing myself, getting injured and mashing myself up for nothing. 'If you move out of here one more time to go training', he ended, 'don't come back.' Scenes like this will strike a chord with many aspiring black sportsmen. For very many black parents, sport is considered to be idling your time away. Strangely enough, sport is not the overriding tradition of the West Indies. In Jamaica they say, 'By the sweat of your brow, you should eat bread.' It is a biblical saying and a favourite of my father's.

Yet there is some running background in my family. Mum

ran when she was young and my two elder sisters, Lorraine and Lisa, could have been good. Russell, my younger brother, also showed some promise but was hindered by a knee problem. In those days, of course, there wasn't much money at all to be made from athletics. A golden few could collect handouts in brown envelopes in hotel rooms around Europe and that was it. Today the climate is totally different and a number of us can make some money from athletics – enough, at least, to enable us to devote all our time to it. In addition, athletics is a very high-profile sport, and so maybe the new, younger generation of black athletes can profit from that and gain the encouragement of their parents.

I can think back to my very earliest days in Britain. After church on Sundays I used to race Dad to the bus stop. In the beginning he would always win and then one day, inevitably I suppose, I beat him. After that he didn't want to race me any more! We were just father and son having a good time. I don't think that he ever imagined I would take up running so seriously. Now, he is one of the proudest parents in the world.

Cosford is a Royal Air Force station on the fringes of the wild Wenlock Edge. It is a surprising place to find the main indoor athletics stadium in Britain, housing a 200 metre indoor synthetic track and, for the biggest events, enough seating for 5000 people, in one of its great hangars. Visiting teams from the Soviet Union, United States, German Federal Republic and France all stare bemused on arrival, and they become even more astounded when told it is the only indoor facility in the country.

In the late seventies and early eighties, travel to Cosford could sometimes be likened to a cross-polar expedition as athletes and spectators battled through blizzards and packed snow, up or down the M6 and along the A5, or up the A41 from Wolverhampton. By rail you could alight at the tiny wooden platform that has been used by servicemen for decades. Now the bell is beginning to toll for indoor athletics at the station as, at long last, new facilities are being opened, at Kelvin Hall in Glasgow and soon at the big centre in Birmingham. But for many, Cosford will always be the home of British indoor athletics, and the first meeting of any year is always the Cosford Games.

I made my second journey to Cosford in 1980, an Olympic year – though I had no aspirations in that direction. My first appearance had been in the Junior Indoor Championships the previous year, when I had been eliminated in the heats. I was determined to do better this time. I ran in the Cosford Games 60 metres and finished third. Two weeks later I lined up in the 200 metres, one tight-bended lap of the track, in the AAA Indoor Championships, again meeting Phil Brown. Surprisingly I was the oldest in the race at nineteen, so the statisticians tell me. This time I finished third and this earned me my first indoor international, with a place in the 4 × 200 metres relay team, against West Germany. It was not, in all honesty, an auspicious debut.

We ran the race as if we were competing in a 100 metres, charging full tilt at the bends. Mike Powell was handing over to me and in the general mêlée of the race he had run out of his box and I had run out of my lane, so we were disqualified twice! I was mortified, because we didn't appear at the presentation ceremony and I didn't receive a medal as a memento of the occasion. Later, Lynn Davies, who was the team manager, gave me the medal. It meant a lot to me and was a fine and understanding gesture by Lynn.

In May, at the start of the outdoor season, I won my first Middlesex Senior title at 100 metres. The time was 10.6 seconds, which was my fastest legal time to date (that is, the wind speed was below 2 metres per second) and would turn out to be my fastest that year. It often happens, especially if you train only spasmodically, that you start off the season with a personal best time, get really excited because you think there is a lot more to come and then the rest of the summer turns out to be something of a damp squib. I finished third in the Inter-Counties Championships. Harry King, the winner, was an established athlete, fast out of the blocks and with a very good technique. Second was Ernest Obeng, who a year later in Rome was to finish second in the World Cup 100 metres behind Allan Wells. There were lessons all around me about what I should be doing, where I should be going, but I chose to ignore them. I made only the semi-finals of the Olympic Trials. I wasn't really disappointed at all; I had a devil-may-care attitude to my athletics. I was enjoying running but was still not going to put in the time necessary to break into the top rank. I was not prepared to suffer in any shape or form in training.

The year of 1980 turned out to be a great one for British sprinting. Great Britain had in the previous eighty-four years of modern Olympic history produced only one 100 metres champion, Harold Abrahams, who had won in Paris in 1924 at the Stade Colombes. Now it had produced a man who seemed capable of duplicating that feat in the vast Lenin Stadium in Moscow.

Allan Wells was born in Edinburgh in 1952. He dabbled in the long jump until the age of twenty-four and then decided to switch to the sprints. But that was in 1976, a black year for British sprinting when no one was selected for the 100 metres at the Montreal Olympics. Four years later, aided, encouraged and finally coached by his wife Margot, the dour, muscular Scotsman was ready, his chances enhanced considerably by the absence of three American sprinters, Stanley Floyd, Mel Lattany and Harvey Glance, all suffering from the ill-conceived and, in the end, totally purposeless American boycott of the Games in protest at the Soviet invasion of Afghanistan.

The Olympic final turned out to be a battle between Wells and the Cuban Silvio Leonard. At the end it took a photo-finish camera to separate them, the Scotsman winning the verdict in 10.25 seconds. It was a great triumph and a turning point in British sprinting history. 'If Allan Wells can do it,' British sprinters said to themselves, 'so can I.' The benchmark had been set.

4
In Limbo

The year 1981 saw the beginning of a breakthrough for me. At the Cosford Games I won the 60 metres, my first major senior success above county level. Two weeks later I won my first national title at the Indoor Championships, taking the 200 metres. It was an exultant feeling, climbing on to the rostrum, waving to the crowd and receiving my medal. In addition, I had equalled Peter Little's record with 21.8 seconds. When you consider that these days we are running well over a second faster, your can see by how much British sprinting has advanced.

Winning the title meant that I was selected for Great Britain to run against West Germany in Dortmund. It was quite an occasion in more ways than one, for I had not travelled abroad since my arrival in England back in 1967. It meant that I had to renew my Jamaican passport. We had never been able to afford to go on holidays – Dad had had to work all the time – so school holidays had been spent at home. I remember that at primary school we had to keep a diary, and from time to time someone would be picked out to face the class and read it aloud. I used to listen to other children describing holidays in Bournemouth or Butlin's or Benidorm, and not wanting to feel out of it I used to invent mine because I had never been anywhere!

I thought that I would wear my Great Britain tracksuit to the airport. I really fancied myself doing that, but Mum would have none of it. She made me put on my suit and collar and tie. I tried to sneak out with an open-necked shirt, but she called me back. On the train I met Peter Little. He had on ripped jeans, a sweatshirt and an old pair of training shoes. When we got to the airport Shirley Strong said to me. 'Hey Linford, have you just come from work?' I was really embarrassed.

I had an excellent run against the Germans, winning the race in a new British record of 21.7 seconds. I was really excited, believing that I was going places. I wanted to compete everywhere, especially at the match against the German Democratic Republic at Cosford a fortnight later.

Unfortunately there was to be no 200 metres event, but there were some invitation events scheduled including a 60 metres, and having won that event at the Cosford Games I thought that I would be selected. I asked Frank Dick, the Director of Coaching, about this but all he said was that the field for the 60 metres had been chosen (by him, as it turned out). I was perplexed. I had beaten some of the sprinters selected for the invitation 60 metres and yet Frank Dick didn't want me to run. He gave no reason, just reiterated that there was to be no 200 metres. Even though I was earning only £20 a week (before tax) at that time, I would have paid to run in that race. I was really disappointed.

On the flight back from Dortmund I talked to Lynn Davies, who was again our team manager, about the problem. Lynn told me not to worry, that he would sort it out with Frank. At Heathrow Wendy Hoyte was being met by her husband Les and they were going to give me a lift back into London. Just as we were about to leave, Frank Dick called me to one side and gave me a blistering reprimand. 'How dare you go behind my back,' he said. 'It's my job to decide who runs in races and who doesn't. How dare you ask somebody else if you can run when I say you can't. If I say no, then it's no.' He was extremely angry.

Frank has since denied this story, but it has stayed vividly in my mind ever since. It was the first time that anybody had ever spoken to me like that and I was shocked. At the time my athletic naïveté was such that I didn't even know what a Director of Coaching was. But whatever it was, from that moment on I had no respect for it. I was angry, too; we were adults and shouldn't be treated like schoolboys.

As it turned out, I went to Cosford and did run the 60 metres. I was determined to do well, in part to say thank you to Lynn Davies. He was a top international athlete, an Olympic champion. I didn't have to explain to him how I felt; he knew. All I wanted to do was run for my country, to be part of the action. After my run at Dortmund I was full of excitement and confidence. I just wanted to compete any time, anywhere. I ran third. Peter Little won the race and Andy Pitts came second, but I had beaten three others who had originally been selected ahead of me, including Cameron Sharp, who the following year was to have a great outdoor season. More importantly, I ran 6.87 seconds for a personal best. I felt I had fully vindicated my request.

This incident set the pattern for my relationship with Frank Dick over the ensuing seven years. At times it has been acrimonious to an extreme and very public. Our personalities are different, and we rub each other up the wrong way almost immediately. I believe that Frank is too autocratic, too opinionated – especially about relay selections, which have been the main bone of contention between us down the years. I believe that he is second to none as a theoretician, but coaching requires much more than that. It requires a depth of human understanding, an ability to communicate on a one-to-one basis with different characters, and I do not believe that Frank can do this very well. After Dortmund, Lynn Davies understood how I felt, knew what was fair; Frank didn't.

I mentioned earlier that just when you thought that the moment had arrived for Mike McFarlane to make a breakthrough he had a setback, and in 1981 this applied also to me. I had had a very successful indoor season, set a British indoor record at 200 metres and a personal best at 60 metres, and gained my first individual international selection. I seemed all set to continue my way to the top outdoors, but as it turned out, the highlight of my summer was getting my photograph in *Athletics Weekly*, the bible of the sport, for the first time.

I was still lackadaisical about my training, still playing dominoes in Mick's café when I should have been out running repetition 300 metres on the West London track. I am sure that I was the despair of Ron's coaching life, but still he made no comment. I took long breaks away from training and would then reappear like the proverbial bad penny, as if I had never been away. My 100 metres time didn't improve at all that year, and it took me until September to better my indoor 200 metres best outdoors when I ran 21.6 seconds at Woodford Green. In the AAA Championships there were very tough qualifying conditions, only the first in each heat going through to the final. With people in the field such as Don Quarrie and a Mike McFarlane near the peak of his form, I would have had to better my best by a considerable margin to succeed. I was duly eliminated.

The year 1982 was an important one in athletics, with the Commonwealth Games in Brisbane and the European Championships in Athens. A year earlier in the World Cup meeting in Rome, British sprinting had received a tremendous fillip when Allan Wells, running for Europe, won the 100 metres, with tiny Ernie Obeng who, though representing Africa, lived in Britain, coming second. Wells had also had the intense satisfaction of beating the Americans in winning the IAAF Golden Sprint title in Berlin.

Wells won three medals at the Commonwealth Games. In the 100 metres he beat the emerging Canadian sprinter Ben Johnson; in the 200 metres, in one of the most exciting events of the whole meeting, he tied for the gold medal with Mike McFarlane, and in the relay Scotland gained the bronze.

These were curious times for me. I was in a kind of athletic limbo, in between national championship class and true international standard. I suppose I lacked serious ambition. I had discovered parties, wine and women, much to the chagrin of my parents and coach. The year 1982 was, perhaps, a matter of what might have been. I reached the final of the AAA Championships at Crystal Palace. I had set a personal best of 10.5 seconds in my semi-final, and was running into silver-medal position in the final when my hamstring went. The winner, Cameron Sharp, clocked 10.31. Earlier in the year I had improved my 200 metre time down to 21.2. My season ended early.

The season of 1983 began with another skirmish with Frank Dick over my non-selection for the European Indoor Championships. I was second at Cosford to Earl Tulloch, 21.9 seconds to his 21.7. The British Board had the opportunity to take two people for the event but, presumably on Frank's recommendation, they elected to take only one. Earl was eliminated in the opening round. Ron wrote Frank a letter of protest, but of course it was too late.

There is a curious meeting held at the beginning of each season called the United Kingdom Championships, which actually is an event to cater for the up-and-coming athletes and bears no relation to a British championship. In recent years there has been an improvement in the standard and a number of top athletes have appeared at the event to earn it some respectability. In 1983 it was held in Edinburgh and I was among the entries. I had won the Middlesex 100 metre title, having moved back to Thames Valley Harriers. The County Championship was a big meeting in those days, with intense rivalry between west and north London. John Isaacs, the coach of Mike McFarlane, had moved his squad over to Haringey, away from Victoria Park Harriers because of alleged racism, so the sprints occasioned greater interest than usual.

Buster Watson was expected to win the 100 metres, but I came through and clocked 10.4 seconds for a personal best and a county record, which still stands. So it was with some hope that I travelled to Scotland. I made the final, along with Buster and a big local star, Drew McMaster. I was feeling in really good shape and very confident. It was a wet and windy day and I warmed up a little more carefully than usual. Then there was a dispute between two athletes, Colin Gaynor and Steve Eden, as to who should be in the final, because they had both qualified as fastest losers with exactly the same time. This held up the whole meeting and finally it was decided to postpone the event for over an hour, so we all left the track.

We all had to warm up again later and I didn't have the necessary background for that; when we finally ran, Buster was the winner, Drew second and I came in third. However, the run earned me my first individual outdoor international selection for a match against Finland at Lappeenranta. It was the year of the first World Championships, and many of the big names in sprinting were biding their time. I won the 100 metres in 10.46 seconds, beating Drew. I developed a sore hamstring but still ran the relay in which we were disqualified, much to Frank Dick's very obvious disgust. Drew then withdrew from the 200 metres and I was asked to run. I demurred. I had my problem hamstring and knew that I hadn't had the necessary training to run a 200 metres after a 100 and a relay.- Pressure of the 'If you don't run then you won't be selected again' variety was not very subtly exerted, so I ran, coming in third behind Donovan Reid and a Finn.

It was the first time that I had experienced the midnight sun. The match was on 18 June, almost the summer solstice, so most of us had to try to sleep with our pillows over our heads. The coach journey the next day to Helsinki airport was very long, and when I stood up to get off I finally pulled my hamstring. It was the end of my 1983 season.

Ron was still coaching me, when I took the trouble to turn up. My domino playing was at its peak and all that I was achieving was gained through natural talent. I took a lot of time off, always after the indoor season, and returned smiling in the summer. Ron finally became angry and wrote me a letter asking when I was going to turn up for training. I ignored it and carried on taking a long break. A second letter followed, which said tersely, --'If you don't come back and train – forget it.' How he had put up with my attitude for so long is a mystery to me. He is a quiet, unassuming man who prefers to let his athletes do his talking for him. He is always there at West London Stadium, three times a week, in all weathers, quietly supervising the work of his athletes. Coaches like Ron are the unsung heroes of British athletics.

I had left the Co-op and joined the Civil Service as a clerical assistant in the Tax Office. It was the biggest mistake of my life and one that I really try hard to forget. It was utterly dull and repetitive, day after day of filing for the Inland Revenue. The woman in charge was a martinet who treated all those beneath her like children. The biggest excitement was receiving your birthday rise which, in the end, worked out at about fifty pence. Progress was slow, security of tenure was all. I use to dread going in to work – in the two years I worked for the Inland Revenue I do not think I worked a full month – and in the end I left. For someone of my temperament it was the worst possible kind of job, and towards the end I was beginning to feel suicidal.

After a comparatively quiet two years my athletics career came alive again in 1984, Olympic year. It started all wrong with an aggravating incident indoors when I was to run against the American Mel Lattany and Earl Tulloch. I was given the inside lane and I was furious and protested. My anger increased when the meeting Director, Len Smith (who fancied himself as a pocket-sized version of our trenchant promotions officer Andy Norman), said to me, 'If you don't run, you'll never run again. You are here to entertain the public.' I swore at him. 'I'm here to run for myself,' I said. 'What do the public know or care about when I'm out training in the cold; what do they care when I am injured?'

Ron said that I should not go on to the track and kill myself because I might pull a hamstring. We both knew that if you draw – or more likely have drawn for you – lane 1 then you stand no chance. Ben Johnson running against a normal standard athlete would not win from lane 1. I jogged round in 23.2 seconds, a trifle faster than Simmone Jacobs ran in the women's event.

I opened the outdoor season in style, beating Mike McFarlane in the Middlesex Championships. The significance of this became clear later, because this was one of Mac's great seasons, when he reached the Olympic final in Los Angeles. A week later we met again in the United Kingdom Championships in Cwmbran, in south Wales. It was the last weekend in May and the weather was cold and windy, the norm for this meeting. Although I did not relish such conditions I reached the final quite easily; but then disaster struck. The starter called us to our marks, we got set, the gun went off and I dawdled on the blocks. The whole field left me for dead. McFarlane won it in an extraordinary 10.08 seconds, gale assisted. I finished sixth in 10.31, also gale assisted. The summer had arrived so I was training more regularly, but still lightly. The run at Cwmbran exemplified my attitude. If I couldn't win, I thought, what is the bloody use of trying? So I just didn't bother.

In June came the Olympic Trials at Crystal Palace. There was pre-selection, and only the winner from this meeting would be selected. Allan Wells, as defending champion, had already been selected. McFarlane won the race and earned selection, while I finished fourth.

There was still a chance to earn a place on the Olympic team; the final place would be decided at the AAA Championships at Crystal Palace. I felt that my running was improving as the season progressed and that I was in with a chance. As it turned out, Donovan Reid won and I came second, missing the third individual place but feeling that I was in with a chance of making the relay team. I won the U-Bix Copiers massive ten-man race at Birmingham, so I asked Frank Dick if there was a chance for me to get in the relay team, which hadn't been announced with the main selections. He told me that if I kept running well, I was in with a chance. The individual sprinters were Wells, McFarlane and Reid for the 100 metres and Buster Watson and Ade Mafe, a new talent, for the 200 metres.

In the end I didn't get picked. Britain usually send six or seven for the relay team but for Los Angeles the selectors decided to rely on the sprinters that had been picked for the individual events. I was extremely disappointed, but didn't make a fuss. I just carried on training and waited for the team to return from America and the post-Olympic meeting at Crystal Palace. There was a world-class field: McFarlane and Reid, the Olympic finalists, Lincoln Asquith, Ernie Obeng and Cameron Sharp. I was in lane 1, and when the television commentators introduced the field they started in lane 2. I won in 10.44, my fastest electrical time.

I went back to West London Stadium where there was a portable television set, and a lot of Thames Valley athletes were crowded around watching a recording of the meeting. When they saw me winning, the clubhouse went crazy with people cheering and whooping. I felt wonderful, and it was at that moment that I realised that if I started taking my athletics seriously, if I started training properly, if I started listening to Ron, then maybe I could do something in the sport.

There had been in 1983 and 1984, two great festivals of athletics: the first ever World Championships in Helsinki and the Olympic Games in Los Angeles, respectively. The first saw every athletic nation in the world represented, the second a retaliatory boycott by most of the nations of the Eastern Bloc.

The inaugural World Championships was the finest track and field meeting that the world had ever seen. Its star was the American Carl Lewis, who won three gold medals – in the 100 metres, long jump and sprint relay. The United States had a clean sweep in the 100 metres with Lewis being followed home by Calvin Smith and Emmit King, but Lewis was totally predominant, winning by almost two metres. A semi-finalist in the event was a young Canadian, Ben Johnson. Allan Wells finished fourth for Britain in both the sprints; Cameron Sharp reached both semi-finals.

In the razzmatazz of Los Angeles Carl Lewis went one better, emulating the feat of the legendary black athlete Jesse Owens in the 'Nazi' Olympics of 1936. He won four gold medals, adding the 200 metres to the three titles he had won in Finland. Ben Johnson was getting closer to the man who would be his great rival, winning the bronze behind Sam Graddy but ahead of two British sprinters, Mike McFarlane and Donovan Reid. Wells finished a sad eighth in his semi-final. In the 200 metres Britain's sole representative, teenager Ade Mafe, finished eighth. He was about to embark on temporary fame, not unaided by the fact that his coach, Ken Seddington, was Benny Hill's television stand-in.

5
Hope and Despair

Andy Norman is the Promotions Officer of British Athletics and the man mostly responsible for the extraordinary rise of the sport during the late seventies and throughout the eighties. Promotions, the staging of major international meetings, the temporary importation of foreign stars, negotiations with television, the whole wheeling and dealing is his business. More than that, it is his raison d'être.

Andy is a street-wise ex-cop, with a blunt, no-nonsense approach that is offensive to some but appreciated by many. His reputation is world-wide and surmounts language barriers. Speak to a Kenyan distance runner in the high hills of the Rift Valley, a Bulgarian hurdler, a Soviet pole vaulter or even a Chinese high jumper and though they may not understand a word of what you are saying, when you utter the words 'Andy Norman' lights will shine in eyes and heads will nod in recognition and they will search, sometimes desperately, for an interpreter.

It all began for Andy in the mid seventies when he staged international 'spectaculars' and England matches, mostly at Crystal Palace but also at Gateshead. The man who ushered in a golden age of middle-distance running, Brendan Foster, was at the peak of his powers and the two men who were to carry it to the greatest heights, Steve Ovett and Sebastian Coe, were just beginning to emerge. Andy also struck a chord with foreign stars, such as New Zealanders Rod Dixon and John Walker, and they and the British runners became bargaining counters in hard negotiations across Europe, from Oslo to Zurich, from Brussels to Nice. Athletics had never seen anything like it.

He has an uncanny eye for spotting talent and then displays a willingness to nurture it. Sometimes he will show a kindness and tenderness that would amaze those who see only the hard, fairly ample exterior, the product of twenty years of police work. If an athletics official can be such a thing, he is a legend in his own lifetime.

In the autumn of 1984 I received a personal letter from Andy Norman. He said that I had the ability to be not only Britain's top sprinter but also number one in Europe. He also said that I would have to become dedicated, my lifestyle would have to change and, most importantly, that I must set my sights high. What he wrote was true. I was an avid party-goer, often coming home with the milkman, and a devotee of rum and blackcurrant, and Babycham. I liked the good life, had a happy-go-lucky attitude. I was also the bane of Ron Roddan's life.

I was totally staggered at receiving the letter and sat down and stared at it. For Andy Norman, the king-pin of British athletics, to take time out to write me a personal letter was amazing. I remember thinking that if Andy Norman believed I could be Europe's top sprinter, if he had such faith in me, well then maybe I could. In those days Andy was the celebrated hard man, the subject of many whispered curses. I can remember being invited by him to Crystal Palace and I was just leaving the house, with my bag lovingly packed by my Mum, when the telephone rang. It was Andy's unmistakable voice. 'I've given your lane away,' he said. 'Don't bother to turn up.' That was all. I was mortified and hurt, but that was Andy.

I replied to his letter to say thanks for believing in me, and that I would do my best not to let him down. I didn't get over it for some time; it had touched my heart. When I look back now I realize that it was a big turning point in my career.

Ron, too, was laying down the law. He knew the potential that I possessed but had refused to acknowledge. He gave me an ultimatum: either get down to training properly or we part company. The time had come for me to grow up.

Other changes were also occurring. I experienced tears of real grief for the first time when my granny died. She had been the rock of our whole family, the matriarch, a marvellous, marvellous woman. She had been a major influence in my life, and helped me through the rough patches. When I was debating with myself whether to take up athletics full time I decided, on the spur of the moment, to go up to Nottingham to talk to her about it. We argued, but in the end she said, 'If that's what you really want to do, then do it.' She was the first person to say to me, 'Don't go through life saying, if only . . .' It made up my mind for me.

She had enormous strength of character. Up until the end she did everything herself, always walking alone even though she was over ninety years of age. She had a premonition that she was going to die, and she did so peacefully. Her arteries simply gave up. When we heard that the end was very near we drove to Nottingham straight away, but arrived just too late. The whole family was completely devastated.

I still miss her and think about her almost every day. I remember her gentleness and her firmness. I remember listening, fascinated, to her enormous fund of stories of the old times in Jamaica, of my grandad, whom I never knew, and of the 'white folks'. When granny died an important part of our family heritage went with her.

I left home by mutual consent! I felt that I had to leave. As long as you live in your parents' home you are a child, their child, and they will treat you as such. It is difficult to gain their respect as an adult. Behind you are more than twenty years of habit-forming obedience to the house rules – and why not? It is, after all, their home.

Mum and Dad are staunch Pentecostal church-goers, and will be all their lives. The vast majority of black people go to church; it's a way of life that goes way back. Many of the great black singers began in their local churches. At one time I was very religious, also a regular church-goer. I enjoyed it and I think I am a better person for it. Having a faith makes you feel very relaxed with yourself and with life. But I stopped going to church around 1983. It was a gradual thing, assisted by the fact that I went training on Sunday mornings. This doesn't mean that I have stopped believing, but only that I believe in my own way. I still pray to God to help me before every race. I realize that there may well be seven others doing exactly the same thing, but I believe that God will help the most sincere and the most deserving.

Dad urged me to move out. Most parents, and not only black ones, are steeped in their old traditions, the old ways of doing things. But life moves on, times and lifestyles change and it is difficult for some to change with them. 'Man has to look after woman,' is my father's philosophy. What has to be, has to be.

So, while they would never encourage my sisters to leave, they made it clear that my time had come. 'Time you got up,' Dad said, 'and got going.' It was just like a fledgling leaving the nest to find its own worms.

Dad taught me a lot as I grew up. He is a good cook, believing that it is important for men to learn to cook so that if they marry a woman not too well versed in the culinary arts, they will still survive! I began to learn to cook in Jamaica at my grandmother's side, watching everything she did. My mother told me I was more domesticated than my sisters. All this may seem a little behind the times to the modern generation and to feminists, but I recognize that it was the way of my mother's and father's world.

I haven't yet married and am not in a rush to do so, so I suppose that in this regard I am a disappointment to my father, though I'm sure he understands that it would be unfair for me to marry with my present commitment to athletics. One day I will settle down, as they say, and raise a family and I look forward to it, for basically I am a home-loving person.

The 1985 European Indoor Championships in Athens was my first major international meeting, and it showed. The stadium was a new showpiece for the Greeks, but it was vast and awe-inspiring to me and I was totally overcome by the occasion. There were tough qualifying conditions in the heats: the first in each heat automatically and then a number of the fastest losers. I was made even more nervous by the fact that the Italian Stefano Tilli, who had set a new world record of 20.52 seconds earlier in the season, was in my heat. We lined up – I had never seen so many people in a stadium in my life – the gun went and I spent just over twenty embarrassing seconds in Tilli's slipstream. I failed to qualify: Ade Mafe just made it, but only got as far as the semi-final. That day I made a vow to myself that I would return to Athens and run better. I also made a promise to myself that when I got picked again for a major championship I would progress beyond the first round.

The United Kingdom Championships were in Antrim in Northern Ireland that year. The weather was appalling, torrential rain, heavy winds and icy temperatures – ideal for sprinting! I remember thinking on the Sunday, as Ian Paisley stood outside the ground and tried to bring the wrath of God down upon us for violation of the Sabbath, that maybe he was succeeding. For many of us it was our first time in Northern Ireland and we were nervous about the Provos and the troubles. At night, in our hotel, we practised how quickly we could roll out of our beds in case of an attack! But despite all this I had a successful Championship, winning the 100 metres and tying, in an exciting race, with John Regis in the 200.

I had been training throughout the winter and Andy, as promised, sneaked me some races in the summer. He sent me back to Lappeenranta with a distance runner, Steve Harris. 'Don't tell anybody you're going,' he said. 'Just go.' I learned more about distance running and Steve's part in it on that trip than ever before or since. I had a successful run, winning in a windy 10.2 seconds.

They made us leave the hotel very early in the morning for the trip home. For some reason which escapes me we had to take a taxi, and when we arrived at Helsinki airport we had to wait five hours for our flight. Andy had given us a special ticket which was non-transferable, so we sat in the departure lounge disconsolately watching half-empty flights leaving for Heathrow. When we returned I spoke forcefully to Andy about the matter. Quite rightly, he exploded.

'Who on earth do you think you are?' he said. 'You couldn't fill a telephone box! When you can put bums on seats, then you can come and tell me what flights you want to travel on. Until that time be happy with what you can get.' It was vintage Andy.

Ron and I continued to search for races. I raced against Cameron Sharp a number of times and beat him, so it was galling to find a few weeks later that he was racing Carl Lewis on the Continent. We persevered. I was the first home for England in the match against the USA at Birmingham's Alexandra Stadium, overhauling Lincoln Asquith and Mike McFarlane in the second half of the race after a poor start but failing to catch the Americans Morris and Cook. Again the weather was cool and wet, with a strong headwind against us. The same applied a week or so later when I won the 100 metres at Gateshead against France and Czechoslovakia. I clocked 10.42 seconds, a legal best for me, but what we needed most of all were sunshine and warmth. It is amazing that we produce any sprinters at all in this country, when you consider the conditions under which we have to race and train.

So we came to the AAA Championships. It was the first Championships where athletes could receive subventions (appearance money paid into a trust fund for the athlete). This, of course, did not affect me at the time! It was also the Championships where more titles went abroad – thirteen – than ever before. The 100 metres turned out to be a controversial race. Chidi Imo, with whom I was to have some great races in the future and who became a friend, was in the thick of the arguments. In the semi-final, in which I ran second, Cameron Sharp was in the lane adjacent to Chidi, who has a side-to-side action with his running which many felt made Cameron run along one of the lines so that he was disqualified. Frank Dick was not happy, and it did seem a harsh decision.

In the final Mike McFarlane was drawn adjacent to Chidi and he also was disqualified, for the same offence as Cameron. Add to that a lot of nervousness which led to two false starts, and nobody was too happy, except perhaps Ernie Obeng who just pipped the American Darwin Cook to win. I was least happy, because again I sustained a hamstring twinge and pulled up. It was the second time I had failed to finish an AAA Championship and I vowed to do better.

I was now increasingly worried about my recurrent hamstring injuries, the treatment of which was costing a lot of money, paid for by parents and girlfriend. But luckily help was at hand in the person of Anna-Lisa Hammer, a blonde, Norwegian freelance journalist who was also the Press Officer for the Bislet Games in Oslo. I had met her at the England–USA match in Birmingham and she had offered to help me with my career. I had told her I was struggling, had no sponsors and no Sports Aid Foundation help. At the time I had a job as youth worker at a sports centre in Acton. I telephoned Anna-Lisa after the AAAs and told her about my injury. 'Come to Norway,' she said, 'and we'll get it fixed.' People later thought that she was my manager, but we were just good friends. She simply loved athletics and wanted to help. I went to Norway and she paid for my treatment. I saw an excellent physiotherapist and a chiropractor who subjected me to some tests and found that the ratio between my hamstrings and my quadriceps wasn't good enough. I also found that I had a vitamin deficiency, and Anna-Lisa introduced me to vitamin supplements. At the end of it all I felt a great sense of relief and well-being, and now I always go to Norway for treatment.

I have a lot of respect for the people there and for the fact that, at least for me, the treatment I received was really cheap.

When I was fit and well I began thinking about making the relay team for the European Cup Final which was to be held in Moscow. I thought my form had been good enough throughout the year to warrant selection, but there is always that niggling doubt, especially as I had angered Frank Dick by not turning up for a relay practice at Loughborough where he was engaged in running the annual Summer School for athletics. The problem had been that there had been a mix-up over my return tickets from Oslo and I couldn't get back. Anna-Lisa had telephoned Frank to say I would be late and he had said there would be no problem.

I received a letter from the British Board saying that I was a possible selection for the European Cup. The problem was that I still had a Jamaican passport and to run in a major meeting like that it was necessary to become a British subject. Mary Tupholme at the BAAB and the immigration people were really helpful, and I became naturalized in about two weeks. It meant driving up to the London Passport Office a few times and waiting around there for interminable periods, but I hoped that it was going to be worth it.

Meanwhile I was running well, with close races against Cameron Sharp and Lincoln Asquith, but relay teams were an ongoing problem. In 1984 I had run in a makeshift team against the projected Olympic foursome. I had run the anchor leg, but wasn't selected for Los Angeles. After I had finally collected my British passport from Petty France, I bought an *Evening Standard* and found that I wasn't in the team. I was absolutely furious. As it was close by I decided to pay Frank Dick a visit at the Board's offices, so I ran to Francis House, but I was told that he wasn't there. I then went to the Grosvenor Hotel where they said Frank was, but still couldn't find him so returned to the BAAB. He was there in the office of Nigel Cooper, the General Secretary. By now I was fuming. 'Why aren't I in the team,' I asked Frank. 'Why didn't you tell me in Brighton when we met that I wasn't in the team? Why did you let me read about it in the papers? What are the reasons?'

Frank tried to fob me off. 'If you come out and tell a person to his face that he's not selected and why,' I said, 'well, it might hurt but at least you know.'

Then I pushed him. 'The only reason I don't punch you,' I said, 'is that I don't want to come down to your level.'

Nigel Cooper in typical fashion, said, 'Well, Linford, it's good to see that you're angry. It shows you're keen.' I walked out of the office and out of the European Cup.

I talked it all over with Ron. I felt that if ever there was a close selection decision, I wouldn't get it. It seemed that the only way I could be sure of making teams in future was to be so far ahead of the opposition that they couldn't possibly leave me out. It was this burning ambition that I took with me into 1986.

6
Harassment

I well remember the day when I first stared hard, malevolent racism in the face. I believe that I will always remember it, even though it was quite a few years ago and even though it has recurred quite a few times since.

It was early morning and I went down to answer a bang on the front door of Dad's house. I had been in the bathroom and was in my dressing-gown. When I opened the door, three white men stood facing me.

I have never experienced any racism in athletics. We all mix well together, support each other, treat each other as equals. By and large black athletes receive identical treatment to everyone else. Up until this moment of opening the door of Dad's house and looking at these three men, I had experienced very little prejudice in life either. I had heard stories, including horrendous tales of harassment by the police from other people in the black community but my family and I had so far escaped such treatment.

There had been a recent incident involving my younger brother, Russell, who had been at a party and on his way home been accosted by a group of men that he knew, who were in a car. They offered him a lift home. He refused. One of them said, 'Come on Russell are you a man or a boy?' An altercation followed and Russell punched one of the men and ran off. That was the story that Russell later told Dad. Dad was awoken by a telephone call about an hour later, around five-thirty.

'Mr Christie,' said a voice, 'you don't know me but I know you, We have met and I know that you are a good man and a religious man. I am therefore sorry to tell you that I am going to kill your son Russell.'

Dad said nothing. He was too stunned.

'I offered your son a lift home this morning, Mr Christie,' the voice went on, 'and he refused. I told him not to be silly and then he stabbed me. Your son stabbed me, Mr Christie. I know that Russell lives in your basement and I am going to kill him. I stopped the police banging down your door earlier out of respect to you. Tell Russell to give himself up to the police and when they have dealt with him, Mr Christie, I am going to shoot him.' The line went dead.

Dad went down to see if my brother was in his room. Russell told him what had occurred and that he had not stabbed the man but only punched him. Dad looked out of his bedroom window and saw a strange car, with some men in it, parked outside. It drove round the corner and came back. The situation was clearly serious.

My father went to a police station that evening after work to report the threatening telephone call and the fact that his son was being threatened with extreme violence. He spoke to the officer on desk duty who said that a complaint against Russell had been made at another station. Dad gave particulars of his own complaint. The duty officer promised to get in touch but nothing happened for two days. After this a detective saw Dad in the street and said that he wanted to interview Russell. My father said that he would bring him to the station. This was the day before I opened the door to the three men.

I looked at them, all tough-looking, and said, 'Hello, can I help you?'

'Is your Dad in?' one of the men asked.

'No,' I said. I didn't know who was in and who was not, but the incident with Russell and the telephone call had made the whole family wary.

'Mr Christie's not there you're saying,' another man said.

'That's right,' I said.

'James Russell Christie then,' the man said.

I didn't know if Russell was there or not. He is a volatile character, far more so than me, and he came and went as he pleased. I said, 'No.' By now I was extremely suspicious.

The smallest of the group came nearer and said, 'I know you. You're James Russell Christie.'

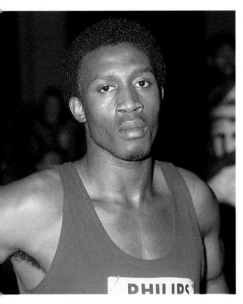

Above: Early days in senior athletics, at the 1980 Philips Night of Athletics at Crystal Palace

Right: 1985 AAA Championships, sprinting against Ernie Obeng (40)

Below: Signing autographs. I'll stay there till the last one is signed

Left: Total elation! My first major win in European indoor championships in Madrid in 1986 beating the Russians Yevgeniev (354) and Roszcanov (363)

Below: Running against the 'Godfather' of British sprinting, Allan Wells. Note the shorts – I did!

Right:
Commonwealth
Games 1986 in
Edinburgh, my
first major outdoor
medal, the silver
behind Ben
Johnson. Mike
McFarlane was
third

Below left: The
height of fashion!
In my Denni Vee
outfit

Below right:
Indoors at
Cosford, ahead of
the 1985 European
Junior Champion
Elliott Bunney

Celebrating in Stuttgart, wreathed in the Union Jack, after winning the 100 metres – first
British winner since 1950

'No I'm not,' I said.

I was grabbed by the lapels of my dressing gown and pinned against the wall. 'You're James Russell Christie,' he said. 'I'm sure that you're James Russell Christie.'

Up until this time no ID card or warrant had been produced. For all I knew these could have been the men behind the call to my father, the men come to shoot my brother. One of the men then gave me a perfunctory glance at a warrant before entering the house and walking up the stairs. I began to grapple with the man who was holding me. Anna, my younger sister, appeared on the landing and screamed. Dad heard her and came down the stairs. I hadn't known that he was in, because normally when he is in the house you can hear him singing and moving around. This particular morning, because his car had broken down, he was unable to take Mum to work and he had decided to have a lie-in. He saw that two men were now holding me, pushing me down and punching me and he recognized the man who was walking up the stairs.

'So,' he said to him, 'this is the way that the police go about their business. You come down here to see me and you beat up my son.'

The moment they realized that Dad was in, they let me go. As one walked outside, another began arguing with Dad who was, naturally, absolutely furious at what had been taking place.

'Linford,' Dad said, 'has absolutely nothing whatever to do with it.'

I went down to the basement to see if Russell was there. He was, with a friend called Tony. I told him that the police wanted to see him. Then we heard a commotion upstairs. There had been a lull. Suddenly the door had burst open and twenty or thirty policemen rushed into the house and began to punch and kick my father. It was obvious that they had been outside all the time, probably in a van. They had blocked the street off, rather as if an armed siege was in progress.

Dad is one of the quietest, mildest men you could meet. He had been in Britain for over twenty years and never had any problem or contact with the police except for one occasion when he was with Mum on a shopping expedition and police officers approached him and said, 'You fit the description of a guy that has just mugged a woman down the road.' Dad had submitted to turning out his pocket and being searched before they let him go. On another occasion he had been struck once by another man at work and we were furious at him for not returning the blow. 'I leave all vengeance to God,' Dad had said and now here he was, nearing sixty years of age, being attacked, in fact, being knocked senseless by the police.

They had come for Russell for his attack on the man in the car. Dad had complained about the threatening telephone call and no action had been taken; but the man had obviously reported Russell to the police and here they were in force to arrest him.

We rushed to join in, to help Dad. I grabbed a chair in a blind panic but heard Dad call out, telling me to put it down. I was kicked in the back in the mêlée. We were all being punched and kicked. Dad was pushed along the passage, into the kitchen. He asked why they were constantly hitting him when he was not retaliating. He was knocked unconscious. When he came round, they dragged him outside and flung him in his night-clothes, into a car and handcuffed him.

I was dragged down the hard, concrete steps on to the pavement. A policeman kicked my testicles hard. 'This one's for Brixton,' he shouted. (Brixton and the riots there were still fresh in everyone's mind.) My dressing gown was ripped. I was flung into a police van, and Russell was also dragged in. He had been handcuffed and was crying with the pain, shouting that they were too tight. They tried to loosen them but failed. Blood began to seep from his hands. The policeman who had kicked me in the groin began to slap Russell around the head. When I told him to stop he laughed. We were taken to the station, dragged down to the cells and left there – all of us, Dad, Russell, his friend Tony and me. Anna had also been arrested in her nightclothes and taken to the station.

I was barefoot and cold; all I had on were my underpants and my dressing gown which, by this time, was just ripped to shreds. I sat there, battered and bruised, very angry and not a little frightened. It was the first time that I had ever seen the inside of a police cell. We were in there for eight or nine hours but it seemed like days. We felt so helpless, so powerless to right what to us was a terrible wrong.

Eventually we were taken up out of the cells and charged. I was charged with three different offences; assault, criminal damage and possessing an offensive weapon. Once the police have arrested you, or so it seemed to us, they will throw the book at you in order to make something stick. They said that I had torn a policeman's tunic. They said that, in the narrow passageway, a corridor whose opposite walls I can touch comfortably with two hands, I had picked up an aluminium chair, ripped it in half, swung it around and hit a policeman with it so hard that he had to shield his head. But he had no injuries that I could see.

They charged Dad with obstructing the police, and claimed that all our injuries had been sustained in the struggle. After we left the police station we all had to go to hospital; we were off work for weeks. In the great fracas in our house, between the three of us and the twenty or thirty policemen, it was our family who were charged with assault.

We attempted to have the case tried in a Crown Court with a judge and jury but it seemed apparent to us, at our first appearance at the Magistrates Court, that every attempt was made, including the dropping of a crucial charge, to keep the case at that level. My solicitor was pessimistic. 'If you are found guilty,' he told me, 'they are going to put you away.'

It was a horrifying time, a nightmare, the future bleak and uncertain. So the stories are true, we told ourselves; there *are* two types of justice in Britain, one for whites and one for blacks. Instances of police racial harassment which had always happened to other people, were now happening to us.

The police gave evidence. One officer said that my youngest sister, who eventually grew to be just 5 feet 4 inches tall but who was still at school at this time, had her arm around his neck trying to strangle him. Another said that Russell had pulled a brick from out of the passage wall and hit him with it. It was impossible that anyone could have torn out a brick through the wallpaper. Even Geoff Capes could not have managed it. Despite this, inevitably I suppose, we were found guilty on all charges. I was fined £100. I found that amazing. I was charged with wilful damage and assault and was fined just £100, equivalent to the penalty for a serious speeding offence. I am sure they thought that if they just gave us a token punishment, then the whole thing would all be forgotten.

We appealed. Again it was a Magistrates Court. The chair I had supposedly used on the policeman had disappeared, obviously thrown away. The police said that they hadn't realized that they had to keep it. The convictions were upheld, the fines stood. The magistrate said that though he acknowledged that Dad was a peaceful, law-abiding citizen who had never had any trouble with the police and who held strong religious beliefs, there were nevertheless times 'when people do get angry and tell lies.' Though they could pinpoint no inaccuracies in our evidence they nevertheless accepted the police's version of events.

The extraordinary irony was that the original case against Russell never reached fruition.

This, my first encounter with real racism came as a shock. In my heart I cannot put down what happened to our family that day to anything else. It still has an effect on me; it is still painful. Every time I think about it, talk about it, it hurts a great deal. Dad, mainly through his strong religious convictions, has forgiven them. He says that if you really believe in God, you have to forgive. But I cannot. To me it was both an ending and a beginning. It was the end of naïveté and the beginning of a hard cynicism, especially with regard to the police.

We were totally inexperienced – greenhorns – as far as this sort of experience went, lost souls entrapped in a web of intrigue. We did not understand the law, we did not understand our rights. But it was only the beginning.

The Christie family then seemed to be marked. Shortly after the case I was walking down the street and a policeman went past, laughed sneeringly and said, 'Got you, didn't we?' Russell had a white girlfriend and the police would approach her and call her 'nigger lover'. So it went on. Dad was under his car working on it one Sunday morning when the police drove by and handed him a 'producer', which meant that he had to go to the police station with all his driving documents.

Near Dad's house there lived a couple. Russell and I were in the road talking whilst he was fixing his car. The husband opened the window of his house. 'Why don't you move away or shut up,' he shouted.

'Excuse me,' I said, 'we are in the street. If you'd like us to move on, come out and talk to us properly.'

This incensed his wife who came out of the house, shouting abuse. Russell, who has a short temper fuse, told her to fuck off. The husband now joined us in the street and the fracas escalated.

'We see you!' the woman screamed at Russell. 'We see you with all those whores you go with!' Russell, now really roused, again told her to fuck off. She attacked him. If I hadn't been there, Russell would have hit her. I held him tight, cooled him down and separated them.

Another woman in the street called the police. When they arrived the woman began crying, behaving as the injured party. We tried to explain the situation as we saw it to the police. They turned to us. 'Listen,' they said. 'Shut up. We don't want to hear from you. In other words, fuck off.'

Two weeks later Russell was arrested for assault. He was remanded in custody for six months. When his case finally came up the evidence of the couple's daughter, who had been watching the whole incident, was torn to shreds by Russell's lawyer. The verdict was not guilty.

A few months later the same man, with his daughter, met Russell at a petrol station. He began the abuse again. Russell ignored him but the ranting went on and finally there was a small exchange. The police arrested my brother again and once more he was placed in remand, this time for four months. But on this occasion, he was lucky because the petrol station attendant had witnessed what had occurred and gave evidence on his behalf. Russell was found not guilty. The judge commented on the fact that Russell had spent ten months in remand for crimes he had not committed.

It was pure, blatant harassment. Altogether Russell had served almost a year in remand and been found Not Guilty on both of his charges. It has made him into a bitter man and I quite understand that bitterness. He has a hatred of the police that will never leave him.

When, in 1986, I collected a new Nissan car that a sponsor had bought for me, I was stopped four times in one day because the car was new and, as I had been told frequently enough by the police when I worked on Ealing Community Relations Council, black men can't afford new cars. It seems to me to be accepted policy to stop a black man driving a new car. The second time I was pulled over I showed the 'producer' I had received from the first policeman, but to no avail. I was still handed a second to cause me extra hassle. This sort of thing still occurs. When I was driving my new Granada in 1989 and dropped a friend down the road, a police car came past, saw the car with a black man driving it, circled round and came back for a second check.

It seems that reasonable cars and the black community, at least in the eyes of the police, do not go together. At one time I had a Morris and on my way back from West London Stadium I dropped off two other athletes in Wood Lane. To do so I drove into a petrol station by the BBC Television Centre in order to do a U-turn. All this time I had been followed by a police car which now stopped. From it emerged a black policeman, who left his white and clearly superior colleague sitting in the car.

'Is this your car?' asked the black cop.

'Yes,' I said.

He went round carrying out the usual checks, asking the usual questions. Are you sure that it is yours? Where did you get it from? Luckily he could find nothing wrong but the disbelief was still in his voice.

'What's the charge?' I asked.

'You were speeding,' he said.

I was sure that I was not speeding. The traffic had been slightly congested there and I couldn't have accelerated to thirty miles an hour. I became annoyed.

'Why didn't your partner come out to talk to me?,' I said. ' I'll tell you why. He sends you out here because it looks impressive.' I felt that I was being used as training fodder for this black policeman.

'If you want to give me a "producer",' I went on, 'then give me one. The reason they recruit, or try to recruit, black policemen like you is that it's supposed to make for better relationships between the black community and the police. But it seems to me to be having just the opposite effect.'

I was angry. My previous experiences had made me wonder if white policemen didn't get a kick out of black policemen investigating black citizens. The cop was embarrassed, and he handed me the 'producer' and left.

'What's a nigger like you doing in an England tracksuit?' the policeman asked. Two officers had stopped me. It was another occasion, another harassment. Gran used to say, 'Just troublesome. Idle hands are the devil's work tools.'

I was on my way home from training, heading towards a fish and chip shop. When I was stopped, I was fed up, angry. Angry with the provocation. We started arguing and round about us were some small children, eager to join in. The argument ended and I went into the shop. One of the policemen followed me in; he looked hard at me. I was still angry and resentful. 'Something smells awful in here,' I said to the man behind the fish bar. As soon as I walked outside, the policeman jumped on my back, twisted my arm behind me and arrested me. There was a scuffle; the other policeman came over and kicked me in the stomach.

'If it's the last thing I do,' I said, 'I'll see you in the street and I'll kick you back.'

They drove me to the police station. I was kept in a cell overnight to appear in court the next morning. I was accused of assault and inciting a riot. I was bound over to keep the peace.

In the summer of 1988 Linford drove to the West London Stadium in the Escort XR3i that Budget Rental had loaned the British Olympic Association for the use of potential team members. Whilst at the track the police arrived and arrested him for being in possession of a stolen car. He was taken to the local police station, charged and bailed out to return at a later date. He received a letter the next day apologizing and accepting that he had not been in possession of a stolen car. At the time of going to press he is taking action but the action has yet to come to trial.

Coincidentally a few days later reporters of the tabloid press began to gather outside his flat, questioning him every time he entered or left. A story appeared in the papers in the usual tabloid style which said that Linford had a secret criminal past and that the police viewed him as a dangerous, vicious character. The Sun *later retracted:*

Linford Christie: Apology

In our July 18 issue we published an article about Olympic silver medallist, Linford Christie, which suggested that a few years ago he was a violent troublemaker who was listed by the police as 'dangerous'. We now accept that the report was based upon inaccurate information and conveyed completely the wrong impression about Linford. We wish to apologize to him, and make it clear, as was pointed out in the article, that he is a man of the utmost integrity who is a good example for kids today.

It would be nice to think that these incidents are isolated but they are not. John Regis, my arch rival at 200 metres, was walking home with some friends late one night when they were attacked by some white men who were obviously extremely drunk. Two policemen were standing across the way and when the attack began John's girlfriend rushed to the police asking for help. They did not move. John and his friend then began to fight back and were gaining the upper hand when the police intervened slamming them up against a wall with their arms pinned behind their backs. The drunks were moved on and John and his friends were followed all the way home. It was his first experience of such blatant prejudice and it came as a shock. In recent years, since he has been successful on the track. John has owned some new cars, firstly an Escort XR3i and in recent months a Mercedes. In the first car he was stopped ten or more times for no reason at all and always asked the same questions: is this your car. . . are you sure that it's your car. . . are you sure it isn't a stolen car, and then asked to produce his driving documents. In his Mercedes he was stopped four times in the first few days. Even affable John, one of nature's gentlemen, can only take so much and has now stopped being polite because when the police recognize him, as they do, they seem to take a particular delight in grilling someone famous.

Mike McFarlane, Commonwealth champion and Olympic finalist, a few years ago before he owned a car, had to travel to the New River Sports Centre on Tottenham's White Hart Lane, where he trained with Haringey. It was a tedious journey, more than one bus ride, often taken at night. Mike would be hurrying along, anxious to get home, carrying his training bag and once a week, sometimes twice, he would inevitably be stopped and be antagonistically grilled: where have you been. . . where are you going. . . what's in this bag. . . training gear, a likely story, and then they would search the bag before reluctantly letting him go on his way.

Kriss Akabussi, World and Olympic finalist, when he was stationed in the Army in Germany brought a new car into Britain and was stopped a number of times on his way to Hampshire.

Most black members of the British team can tell similar stories. For us and the rest of the black community it is a way of life. It makes life difficult. If I want to visit a bank for a few minutes, I park my car as near as possible as many do, to be able to rush in and out again as quickly as possible. Once I did this under the eye of a policeman who nabbed me for parking on a yellow line when I emerged from the bank a few minutes later. Other cars were parked on the lines – it was difficult to find a space! – but I was the driver he chose. So, now, when I visit a bank, I have to think carefully about where I park.

In July, 1989, the Daily Express *reported that ex-Beatle Paul McCartney was funding a Fame-type school on Merseyside through remarks a black friend made to him about the Toxteth riots being mainly caused by police harassment.*

'I had a feeling,' McCartney was reported as saying, 'that what my friend told me was true. I could feel it in my bones. And I have something to back up my suspicions.'

A few years ago, he said, he met an old friend who had become a policeman. He told him he was very excited because he was being posted to Liverpool 8 – Toxteth – and McCartney asked him why.

'I hate nig-nogs,' the friend said.

'I was stunned', said McCartney. 'I couldn't believe that a police-man could have said such a thing. Several years later there was a riot in Toxteth and no one believed it when residents blamed the police. What else am I supposed to think when my school mate was posted to the area especially because he didn't like black people.'

In the end, of course, such harassment of the black community is totally counter-productive. As has been said elsewhere in this book athletics reflects the society in which it exists and the experiences of Linford, his family and black British athletes mirror exactly those of the majority of black British citizens. Total and seemingly irrevocable mistrust builds up, spawned, it has to be said, by racism and totally stereotyped thinking by some members of our police forces. Only society itself can make the fundamental change that is required to make racial harassment a part of history. Only positive action by government in this regard can break down the wholesale and, in many cases, bitter mistrust of the police by black people, for, in the end, complete integra-tion of different ethnic groups is a political issue.

'But I want you to know tonight,' said Martin Luther King in his final and most famous speech in Memphis in 1968, 'that we, as a people will get to the promised land.' Britain, as we approach the second millennium, is far from that place.

I have always disagreed with those in the black community who, when they have applied for jobs and have not been successful, have blamed it on the colour of their skin. 'It's because I'm black' has become the easy, standard excuse.

Often, such people never consider that it might be because they are not academically qualified or had had a bad interview; they automatically blame racism. Sometimes it is, sometimes it isn't, but what black people have to do is to become so well qualified that they cannot be turned down on this basis – or at least if they are they can refer it to the Race Relations Board.

But it is becoming harder and harder to convince them. My experiences lead me to believe that the police can be racist and the British people should be aware of this. Many policemen do appear to have a standard low opinion of black people, are convinced that the majority of the black population are criminal, and believe that a black person is guilty until he can, *if* he can, prove his innocence. And, from my experience, I can only believe that in some measure, the courts are guilty of supporting the police in this attitude, for the sake of maintaining a status quo.

I believe that most of the incidents that I have described will strike a chord with the vast majority of black people. Not many seem to have escaped this type of harassment. Roy Dickens, one of our 400 metre runners, told me that on one occasion he and his brother Brian were shopping with their mother when a white man mugged an old lady and ran off with her handbag. They chased the man, caught him and retrieved the bag. When the police arrived they automatically arrested the Dickens brothers because they were black.

When this type of harassment occurs, when it is continuous day after day, unrelenting in its viciousness, then tensions grow with it and those tensions can creep into the whole community until finally some incident breaks the self-control; the pent-up fury of people is unleashed and often blind, mindless violence occurs. Hence the Toxteth, Brixton and Tottenham riots. I do not of course condone those riots, but I can understand them.

Britain is a multi-racial society. That is a fact of life. People of all races, colours and creeds have to live together, must co-exist. Black people have contributed to the culture of Britain in many ways and black athletes are now an integral part of Britain's athletic success. I am proud to be British, proud to have won honours for all of the people. But when I am kicked in the groin in my father's house, when I am taunted and called 'nigger' and 'black bastard', when I am arrested as a result of police harassment, at those times I am ashamed to be British. And because I am in the public eye it is important that I fight back, that I show the world that the police are not infallible and that the rotten apples in the barrel must be exposed. Obviously I am not saying that all policemen are racist but there seems to me to be enough evidence for a nationwide enquiry into such harassment to be held.

Racism is not part of my makeup. My parents have never been racist, have always preached toleration and moderation, even though, I believe, my father and his family have been abused and dishonoured by the police. That is something I can forgive but never forget.

7

Sweet Success

Determination alone does not get you through life, and these were becoming hard times for me. On my return from Norway I found that the sports hall where I worked had been burnt down. I was redundant and signed on, but it was still hard to make ends meet. I really got embarrassed collecting my dole, and in the end I gave it up. This is where my parents and my girlfriend Mandy were really magnificent; without them I would not have made it into 1986. I stopped going to parties, stopped drinking and threw myself into the regime of Ron's hard training schedules.

Ron Roddan has been coaching at his club, Thames Valley Harriers, for twenty-nine years, first at the Alperton track in north-west London and later at the West London Stadium. A bachelor who is quiet, modest and with a slight stammer, he is wedded to his sport and more particularly to his art, which is the coaching of sprinters. He was a modest sprinter himself back in the fifties and early sixties, once reaching the final of the Middlesex Championships.

'Linford used to like his Saturday nights with his mates,' he said, 'and they affected his Sunday mornings. Sometimes he would turn up, sometimes he wouldn't. I didn't take much notice of him then. If he wanted to join in the group, then he could.'

When the going got tough in training sessions Linford would depart for the canteen. He didn't like and couldn't take the hard training. Ron Roddan was the epitome of patience. 'You have to be,' he said. 'Remember, I had gone through exactly the same business with the Hoyte brothers. They would disappear in the winter and re-emerge with the sunshine. I knew from very early on that Linford had the talent. Although in the early days he was ungainly, he was very tall and rangy, an ideal build for a top-class sprinter. It needed some spark to concentrate his mind, something to take him out of the ruck. Andy provided that, and his non-selection for the European Cup was the final clincher.'

Linford began his first full winter's training. Ron Roddan laughed at the memory. 'He did it,' he said, 'but he didn't like it.'

God, it was tough! All those long nights when I had sat in the canteen I had never realized what was happening just a few yards away on the Tartan track. I hated the cold nights, hated Ron at times, but I kept at it. I ran repetition 300 metres and 200 metres. I pulled heavy tyres along the sprint straight, and I began weight training. So it went on, day after day, week after week, right up until Christmas. Ron was kind; like Mr Scrooge he gave us Christmas Day off.

I opened my competitive year at Cosford as usual, with the Indoor Championships. I ran in a spirited 200 metres and finished third behind Ade Mafe and Todd Bennett. All the press were very excited about Ade, writing that he was our big hope for the European Indoor Championships in Madrid. A couple of weeks later we had an indoor match in Budapest against Hungary and this time I won, 21.3 to Ade's 21.6, with some top Hungarians trailing behind. I thought, well, they were trumpeting Ade for the gold medal. I beat him. Where does that put me? I went to Spain with my confidence sky high. I was also spurred on by Frank Dick's remarks after Ade's win in the Championships. He said that Mafe was the best prospect ever. That hit the right button.

I remembered Frank baiting me at Gateshead the previous year. He had kept making remarks like 'You're not really good enough to make the team' or 'You're not good enough to beat Mike McFarlane and Cameron.' I beat Cameron a couple of weeks later, but didn't see Frank. Such niggling at athletes may be part of some psychological technique that Frank uses. I didn't appreciate it, and I didn't think it worked.

The magnificent Palacio de los Depostes in Madrid was the setting for the 1986 European Indoor Championships. The first European Indoor Games had been held in Dortmund twenty years earlier and at that meeting Britain had provided the winner for the 60 metres in Barrie Kelly. More recently, Mike McFarlane had won the 60 metres the previous year in Athens. Now there was a double challenge in the 200 metres from the young Ade Mafe, Olympic finalist and European Junior Champion, and Linford. The big obstacle to Britain gaining the gold medal was the Russian favourite Aleksandr Yevgeniev, a man who had set a world best earlier in the season and who had beaten Mafe at the initial World Indoor Games in the Palais Omnisports de Paris-Bercy one year before to win the gold medal. In that race Mafe, with 20.96 seconds, had become the first Briton to run under 21 seconds indoors.

I felt totally different in Madrid from a year earlier in Athens. I had a determined attitude, a few months' really hard winter training under my belt and a driving ambition to put behind me the previous year's exit in the opening round. I seemed to be running better and better, more powerfully. Already, I felt, I could feel the benefit of the work I had been undertaking. In each round I had good lane draws and ran comfortably. Ade pulled his hamstring in the first round. In the final, I again had a good outside lane, which was important on this very tight 164-metres track. The draw is everything in a 200 metres indoor race. I had Yevgeniev inside me. Yevgeniev, the King of the Boards, was leading into the home straight but I surged past him to take the gold medal. I felt all sorts of emotions – triumph, happiness and exultancy. I had won my first major title. It was the foremost achievement of my career up until then, and it was the greatest feeling I had ever had.

The commentators talked about a 'surprise' win, and there were hints that if Ade had not had the misfortune that he did, the result might have been different. I don't think that was true. Ade had raced Yevgeniev a number of times before that, in Paris in 1985 and in the European Indoor of 1984, and had never beaten him, and I don't think he would have been ahead of the Russian this time either. It was a great thrill for me to beat Yevgeniev and important for me that he was there. If he had been absent I would have looked upon it as something of a hollow victory.

When I returned to Britain I was buzzing. We had a match against the Russians and I again beat Roszcanov, the bronze med-allist in Madrid. Then there was the grand finale of every indoor season at Cosford, the England versus USA match. Tickets had not been going too well for this event before the European Indoor, but afterwards Cosford was soon sold out. When I next met Andy Norman I said, with a huge grin, 'Remember the guy who couldn't fill a telephone box?' It seemed amazing that it was less than a year since that had been said.

I had a great reception from the public and other athletes at these two meetings. A lot of people seemed genuinely happy for me. It was the first time that I had been picked to run in an individual event against the USA, and I was looking forward to it. I won the 200 metres and the crowd, as always highly supportive of the British athletes, shook the rafters.

I went back into training in a superb frame of mind. I had not only won a major title but my time in Madrid of 21.1 was my fastest ever, indoors or out, and that on a very tight, small track. My running told me that I had been wasting my time all those years, but I didn't regret that too much. Public interest in athletics was growing all the time and it was good to be coming through while that was happening. I now had the incentive to train even harder, and I looked forward to the outdoor season with considerable relish.

After winning the European Indoor I thought that sponsorship and help would come rolling in. They didn't. I was still unemployed and struggling financially, still dependent on my parents and my girlfriend. I telephoned Capital Radio's Helpline, saying that I was Linford Christie and needed help. The man at Capital told me to hold on, and I waited for a very long time. I could just imagine the conversation at the other end.

'There's a guy on the phone says that he's Linford Christie, the European Indoor athletics' champion, and he badly needs help.'

'Yeah? Tell him that if he's Linford Christie, you're the Queen of Sheba. Anyway, those athletes are earning a lot of money these days.'

The man came back to the telephone and said that if I was Linford Christie I was to go in and see them. I travelled in and they did an interview which a fine man called Peter Canham heard on his car radio. He rang Capital and told me to go and see him. Peter owned London Postal Services, and he offered me £5000 and told me to put together a package. I was quite excited and asked Andy Norman to help me. Andy went to see Peter and the final conclusion was that what I really needed was a car to help me travel to training and meetings.

If he had given me the £5000, under the rules at the time I would have had to donate 15 per cent to the British Board – totally unfair in my view as I had had to find the sponsorship myself. The Board said that they deserved their percentage because they had put me in the position to attract the money. I think I'd call that convoluted thinking. Anyway, thanks to Peter I was now a little more secure.

On 3 June I flew into Madrid for a big invitation meeting. I have to thank John Bicourt for being there. John is an ex-international steeplechaser turned entrepreneurial agent, and he and Kim McDonald both do a fine job, mostly for distance runners, in finding all-important overseas competition for British athletes.

Since I was last in the Spanish capital my training had continued on a high plane. Ron had taken us to Lanzarote in the Canary Islands for warm-weather training. It is an ideal centre, with a synthetic track and weight-training facilities very close to the living accommodation. And, of course, the weather is nearly always warm.

Late in May Andy Norman had taken a small party of athletes to Oslo for a meeting. He has close connections there with the Norwegian people, being involved with the two big Bislet meetings and a close friend of Sven Arnie, the promoter. I ran two personal bests, 10.33 seconds for the 100 metres and 20.79 seconds for the 200, which was further encouragement for me and compensation for the traumas I had suffered on the West London track throughout the long, cold, seemingly never-ending winter.

It seemed that all the world and his wife were in Madrid. There was a large American contingent, including Thomas Jefferson, the Olympic bronze medallist at 200 metres, and Emmit King, the 100 metres bronze medallist from the 1983 World Championships in Helsinki. Among the British contingent were Roger Black and Seb Coe with his father–coach Peter. As we stepped out of the plane at Madrid airport the heat hit us like an oven, and that made me feel very good indeed. If there is one thing that sprinters really like, it is hot sunshine!

Some people feel that the herd instinct does nothing for American tourists, and I feel the same about American athletes.

Anna, Mum and Dad – my greatest fans and supporters. To them – and to Gran – I owe everything

At Buckingham Palace being presented with my UK record plaque by the Duke of Edinburgh, President of the British Amateur Athletic Board

Moments I love the most, with budding sprinters at West London Stadium

Left: The art of bend running at Cosford

Below: My friend and frequent room-mate Colin Jackson, Olympic 110 metre hurdles silver medallist in Seoul

Winning a silver behind Ben in the Edinburgh Commonwealth Games of 1986

With my coach, mentor and friend Ron Roddan, the 'quiet man' of British athletics and a great coach

Above: Winning the European Championship in Stuttgart in 1986 ahead of Bringmann of East Germany and Marie-Rose of France

Left: British is best! But I was reprimanded for wearing the flag at the European victory ceremony

Below: Frank Dick, Britain's Director of Coaching. We have had some verbal battles over the years but I valued his help and support in Seoul

Individually they are fine and I get on very well with most of them, but put them together in a group and they seem to have an attitude problem. They feel they are the greatest and they want to flaunt it, as noisily as possible. It isn't my style.

I jogged a few laps with Seb, got really warm and faithfully carried out my stretching routine. This was a new Linford Christie! I felt on top of the world and couldn't believe the heat. I don't think I had ever run in such marvellous conditions. I couldn't help contrasting it with Antrim, Edinburgh, Gateshead, even Crystal Palace where you needed two or three tracksuits just to keep warm.

I chatted to Emmit King before the race. He seemed a really pleasant, friendly man, and I had admired his running before. He was reputed to have a lightning start and had had some close races with Allan Wells.

There were heats, and Jefferson ran in the first. The noise from the stands started: 'Tee Jay! Tee Jay! all the way!' He duly won, and then I lined up with Emmit King for the second heat. Again there was this uproar. 'Go, Emmit, go!' It's odd the memories that can suddenly come into your mind. I remembered being in the weight-training room with two club-mates, Trevor Wade and Clifford Mamba, a few weeks earlier and we had been discussing sprinting. They said that Carl Lewis was the greatest. 'How can he be the greatest,' I asked, 'when he hasn't met me? He has to race against me before you can say that.'

They laughed and jeered and said, 'No chance!'

Emmit King's name cropped up. Mamba said, 'You can never ever beat Emmit King.'

I felt mad and tackled the weights more aggressively. I thought, hell, these guys are supposed to be my friends. Mamba wouldn't let it go. 'Linford,' he said, 'if you beat Emmit King you can come back here and punch me in the mouth; that's how confident I am.' I replied, 'You're on,' and we shook on it.

We settled to our marks, the gun went off and I was away, winning in 10.25 seconds. Emmit was nowhere, way back with 10.7. I was very happy; it was a personal best, and I thought of Clifford Mamba.

We lined up for the final with the usual American din coming from the stands. I didn't lack support; the Spanish public knew me from the European Indoor. I had a moderate start but came through very fast over the last half of the race to win. As I eased down I glanced over at the clock; it read 10.01. I couldn't believe it. No chance, I thought, just my luck the clocks aren't working. Roger Black was going quite berserk in the stands. It seemed ages before they sorted out the time. Then it was announced: 10.04, a new British record. I was ecstatic. Peter Coe rushed up to congratulate me, and people were shaking my hand. The American contingent were mortified. 'A British guy running 10.04,' they were saying to each other. 'Shit! I don't believe it!' It was another good moment.

When I returned to the hotel I telephoned Ron back home in Britain.

'Well, how did you go?' Ron asked.

'I won,' I replied.

'Good. What time?'

'10.4,' I said.

'That's not bad. That's not bad,' Ron said. 'As long as you won, that's the main thing.'

I couldn't keep up the pretence any longer. I was bursting to tell him.

'I'm only joking,' I said. 'I ran 10.04.'

It went quiet for what seemed an eternity.

'Ron, are you still there?' I asked.

'Are you serious?' he said. 'Bloody hell!'

Then the line went dead and I heard the dialling tone. Ron had just put down the telephone. He was totally overcome. I rang back to make sure he hadn't fainted!

I returned to Britain and just shook hands with a very nervous Clifford Mamba.

When I arrived back I found that there had been very little press coverage and quite a lot of disbelief. 'Be reasonable,' some 'experts' were saying, 'can you see Linford Christie running 10.04?' What they hadn't realized was that this was a new Linford, stronger, fitter, faster than ever before and running in really ideal conditions for the first time in his life.

I went to Oslo for the Bislet Games, one of the world's top athletics meetings with the stands always packed and the crowd highly knowledgeable – a tremendous atmosphere. More world records have been set at the Bislet than at any other stadium in the world. It is easy to see why: the track is only six lanes wide so that the crowd is closer to the action than usual, and the organizers have the knack of building up the anticipation for the big event so that once it gets under way, emotion bubbles over. I won the 100 metres, beating a number of Europeans including one of my main rivals for the Championships in Stuttgart, Frank Emmelmann of East Germany, who had won in Athens four years earlier. I was now a serious contender for the gold medal.

It is curious the hold on the public's – and indeed the athletes' – imagination the AAA Championships has. I suppose the expression rolls off the tongue – the three As – and, of course, the meeting goes back over one hundred years. Domestically, it is still *the* title to win. Two days before the 1986 meeting I took my starting blocks home to my flat and left them on the kitchen floor. I came out to get myself a drink and stepped on the edge of the bar of the block, taking a big chunk of skin out of my foot. I panicked. The Championships were very important this year, a selection meeting for the Commonwealth Games and the European Championships. I rushed to see a physiotherapist, John Harris, and he made up a little pad around it with a hole in the middle so that I wouldn't put any pressure on it. Then I went out and bought some anaesthetic spray and applied it, but the pain was so excruciating that I thought my foot would fall off.

I went to the Championships press conference. Most of our major meetings are preceded by these sessions. There was now a big marketing and sponsorship package for the sport, so publicity was important. The AAAs was sponsored by Kodak. I was very relaxed, although I am sure that a lot of the journalists, cynics most of them, were still dubious about my time in Madrid. They were waiting for me to get beaten. Come to that, I suppose, most of the other sprinters were hoping that the timing was wrong and were eager to bring me back down to earth. Despite my little foot problem, I was confident. Also at the conference were two Australian ex-professional sprinters, John Dinan and Chris Perry, who had been running some fast times during the Antipodean summer. Perry, I remember, ostentatiously smoked a pipe and the press became very excited.

The event was held on the Friday night, which is traditional. It is a pity really, because often the weather is cool and the crowd is always small. I cruised my heat and prepared for the semi-final. In the stands, the old north London versus west London rivalry was again hotting up, encapsulated on this evening as Haringey versus Thames Valley Harriers.

I had joined Thames Valley back in the early eighties from London Irish. I think if I have to find a word to describe the club, that word is 'comfortable'. They've always given me tremendous support and, when I've been able to in a busy schedule, I've reciprocated. There are some first-class people in charge, men such as Peter Browne and Laurie Kelly, and you find ex-TVH men popping up at stadia all over the world to give you a shout. I'm totally associated with the 'Valley' now, and it will always be my club.

TVH, as it is generally known, was typified for me by a man called Alf Mignot, who died in 1987 in his early sixties. He had a great sense of humour and was more like a teenager than a man nearing retirement. I remember at Oslo just going to my marks when from the crowd came a shout: 'Go on, Linford! Up the Valley!' It was Alf. He would have been at the Crystal Palace too, willing me on to my first AAA Championship title, revelling in the rivalry, matching the best of the youngsters from Haringey. Mike McFarlane ran in the first semi-final, got away to a brilliant start and was never headed, recording 10.22 seconds. His supporters raised the roof. Les Hoyte, from our club, started taking bets. I ran my semi-final and clocked 10.21 seconds! More bedlam, and in the gathering twilight, everybody looked forward to the final with great anticipation.

Mac got away to a quite blistering start. To this day I have never seen him react so quickly. For a moment I wondered if I would be able to catch him, but it was only for a moment. I came storming through, caught him with about five metres to go and won in 10.23 seconds. Now everyone knew that I had arrived, knew that Madrid had been no fluke. A lot of people, including Daley Thompson, ran personal bests in the final. It was one of the best AAA 100 metres in a long time.

I was the favourite to win the 'double', but in the 200 metres, though I came off the bend in the lead, I relaxed too much and first John Regis and then Todd Bennett came past me. But I still ran 20.51 seconds for a personal best, so I was happy.

I actually felt a different athlete, with a different attitude. Andy Norman and Ron had frequently told me about athletes who were content to be the British number one, to make the team. I hadn't really grasped what they were talking about, but my two successes in Madrid had whetted my appetite. I revelled in winning major titles, setting records; they earned me respect and I wanted more. I wanted to be number one in Europe, the world's top sprinter. In 1986 I cultivated new ambitions which took me out of the British orbit and on to a higher plane. I think, at the Crystal Palace, my sprinting peers suddenly realized that, and it was, for one or two, soul-destroying.

By this time Allan Wells was back in the news again. He hadn't achieved much since his Commonwealth Games gold medals in 1982 and had been eliminated in the semi-finals at the Los Angeles Olympics. He had been sidelined by injury in 1985 and seemed to be playing a cat-and-mouse game with everybody in this year. His name kept appearing in programmes, but then he didn't turn up. He pounced on the Scottish selectors for not picking him for the 4 × 100 metres relay team for Edinburgh and, so it said in one of the tabloids, he was now ready to meet Linford Christie. Allan just had to turn up, so the paper hinted, and I was a beaten man. This annoyed me (I still believed what I read in the papers!). I was still a little niggled at his not congratulating me on beating his British record. When Derek Redmond had broken David Jenkins' long-standing record for 400 metres in 1985, David had telephoned congratulations from California. When somebody breaks my British record, I'll be the first there with my good wishes.

I first met Ben Johnson at the Alexander Stadium in Birmingham just prior to the Commonwealth Games. The press were trying to build up a great rivalry between Ben and me, especially as I had never raced him. I was confident of beating him, but then I believe that you have to be confident of beating everybody. I think that in your mind you should not be second to anyone. My philosophy is that if somebody beats you then he's lucky; that on the day, your best wasn't good enough – but wait for the next time round.

I had just returned from a training stint in Lanzarote. The meeting itself was more like a wake, for more and more athletes were finding out that they were not going to compete in Edinburgh after all because of the boycott that was being staged by the African, Caribbean and Asian countries. The field in the 100 metres was world class with Chidi Imo, the fast Nigerian, Calvin Smith, the world-record holder, and all the top British sprinters. Ben got away to a lightning start and won in a blazing

10.06 seconds; Chidi (not going to Scotland) was second, and I was some way back in third place with 10.32 seconds. My start was beginning to let me down around this time – Ron and I were concentrating more on my pick-up – but I had the satisfaction of beating Calvin Smith quite comfortably. However, I knew the magnitude of the task facing me in Edinburgh.

It was the second time that Edinburgh had staged the Commonwealth Games. In 1970 the Scottish capital had played host to every country entitled to compete in a marvellous celebration of sport. In 1986 it was different for a whole host of reasons, the main one being the boycott, because of New Zealand's sporting links with South Africa, by thirty-two countries. Only twenty-six nations competed. Absent were the great distance runners of East Africa and the sprinters of the Caribbean and West Africa. But there were additional problems. The Scots had failed to appreciate that the organizational structure of sixteen years earlier was now outmoded, and acute financial problems ensued and put the Games on the verge of bankruptcy, facing cancellation with the total humiliation that would mean for Scotland and Britain. The politicians moved fast, and to the rescue came the avuncular, larger-than-life figure of Robert Maxwell, owner of the Daily Mirror *and much else besides. He swiftly put together a package that saved the truncated XIIIth Games.*

In the sprint events the contests would be between the Canadians, the English and the Scots. The favourite was Ben Johnson, the Jamaican-born Canadian, the fastest man in the world in this particular year. Johnson had come on tremendously under his coach Charlie Francis since winning the 100 metres silver medal in Brisbane. He had taken the Olympic bronze in Los Angeles, won the World Cup in 1985 and beaten Carl Lewis in the Goodwill Games in Moscow with 9.95 seconds. Linford seemed assured of the silver medal, which would be England's first at 100 metres since 1938.

It was freezing cold in Edinburgh, and this was July! We were housed on the University campus, some distance away from the town centre. I had heard a lot about Games Villages from other athletes, about the 24-hour restaurants, the recreational facilities, and the great atmosphere. But there was none of these. It was acutely boring, like living in a morgue. All of the first-round heats of the 100 metres were cancelled because of the boycott. Only nineteen competitors turned up.

In the afternoon the event got under way. I cruised the opening heat with 10.32 seconds, beating Desai Williams of Canada and Cameron Sharp. It would have been difficult not to qualify for the semi-final, as sixteen were to go through! The semi-finals typified Meadowbank Stadium. I won my race into a 1.5 metres per second wind. A few minutes later Ben won his, assisted by a 3.11 m.p.s. wind.

Ben sped from the blocks with his usual electric start in the final, and for a while I was behind Desai Williams, but then I started to come through strongly. Then, five metres from the line, I felt a twinge in my hamstring. I eased down, just holding on for the silver medal, but it was the end of my Commonwealth Games.

Now I could set my sights on the European Championships in Stuttgart. I received treatment on my injury every day in Edinburgh, so that by the end I was recovering well. I travelled down to Gateshead for the big meeting there, Great Britain versus the Commonwealth, and was witness to one of the most amazing come-backs in British sprinting history made by, who else, that old war-horse Allan Wells.

The line-up in the sprints was impressive – Ben Johnson, Desai Williams, Atlee Mahorn, Darren Clark, all medallists from Edinburgh, along with Clarence Callender and Mike McFarlane. Allan was representing the Commonwealth, and the second amazing feature of the evening was his attire: tight black cyclist's shorts down to his knees! He looked like an extra from the film *Chariots of Fire*.

He lined up first in the 100 metres. All the pre-race buzz among the 12,000 crowd had been about Ben Johnson. In one of the most extraordinary turn-rounds, Allan swept into the lead, was never headed, and comfortably beat Lincoln Asquith and Desai Williams, clocking 10.4 seconds into a strongish headwind. Ben trailed in fourth. First of all the crowd was stunned, and then they erupted, giving Allan a marvellous reception on his lap of honour. But the night was yet young.

Allan was allowed in as a guest in the 200 metres, but was given the outside lane. Again he dashed away and held on in a close finish with Atlee Mahorn, who was desperately trying to salvage some Canadian credibility out of the evening. I sat in the grandstand, shaking my head. 'I don't believe this,' I kept saying. 'I just don't believe it.' It was pure showbiz, and I noted for later that Allan's shorts, which were similar to those that some Americans and Italians were wearing, had played a not inconsiderable part.

In the cold light of dawn, of course, it was easy to analyse the evening. Many of the champions were suffering from what we might call post-championship blues. You set your sights on a meeting, you build yourself up to it, and naturally what follows can be something of an anti-climax. In addition you start concentrating on the financial side of the sport – you've already got your medal and your title and no one can take that away from you.

In turn, we shouldn't try to take anything away from Allan for that night; he ran really well, a true champion's performance. However, I thought that it was wrong, very, very wrong that he was picked for Stuttgart on the strength of those two races. The selectors let their hearts rule their heads. Allan was due to run in Zurich but he didn't appear, which was absolutely typical, so we still hadn't raced. That was the kind of man he was; he raced when he felt like it. If he felt he wasn't ready then he wouldn't show, regardless of the commitment. Later on in my career, again in the press, he called me a 'sheltered athlete' who kept away from the main opposition. This was nonsense, of course, and in view of his career, rather an impertinence.

The Weltklasse Meeting, established in 1962, in Zurich's Leitzegrund Stadium is one of the truly great meetings of the world where the track and field stars always play to a large and enthusiastic audience of about 25,000 people. It is also the most expensive, but the costs are covered by the worldwide television coverage. Athletes are summoned rather than invited by the promoter Andreas Bruger to perform under the blazing floodlights, and there is rarely a refusal. Television commentators call it the biggest meeting outside the Olympics, and while that is an exaggerated accolade the standard of competition is amazingly high.

The 1986 meeting was no exception. Said Aouita, the highly versatile Moroccan distance runner, was there to attempt to beat the world 3000 metre record. Seb Coe was present to challenge Steve Scott. Evelyn Ashford was to race Olympic champion Valerie

Briscoe-Hooks over 200 metres. Zola Budd, in what was to be her last season, was to resume rivalry with Ingrid Kristiansen and Maricica Puica. Men of the standing of Peter Elliott were relegated to B races – it was that kind of night.

In the sprint events the world's best were assembled. Carl Lewis and Ben Johnson were to resume their rivalry; Chidi Imo was running off his frustration at missing the Commonwealth Games; Calvin Smith, the world-record holder, could always spring a surprise. Linford was there for the first time.

It was my first taste of a major Grand Prix meeting and I thought that it was brilliant, colourful and exciting. It was similar to an indoor meeting because the stadium is compact, with the crowd close to all the action. I didn't realize until this night that the Americans took the Weltklasse so seriously, but I immediately understood why.

Ben told me that Carl had baited him. He went up to him before the meeting and said, 'This is the race that is going to decide between us as to who is going to be the number one.' Ben thought that this was considerable cheek, on two counts: one, he had beaten him earlier in the year in Moscow, and two, Ben had been the faster all year.

We raced. Ben went into the lead at the half-way point and won easily from Chidi Imo and Carl. Calvin Smith came in ahead of me but I beat the Pole Marian Woronin, who had run third at the previous European. I felt that a Ben Johnson made angry by a Carl Lewis had made us all look second-rate. He ran 10.03 seconds into a headwind.

I was, however, pleased with my performance. I had come to Zurich from an 'off' period – it was my first race since the Commonwealth, a gap of about three weeks. Ron was delighted too, saying that I had run well after my lay-off with injury and had beaten one of my main challengers for the European title. Of course, I was also disappointed in not winning. I always am – with me bronze is no good, silver is no good, gold is all. And that now was what I was travelling to Stuttgart determined to win.

8
Golden Stuttgart

The British team of eighty-five athletes left for the European Championships in Stuttgart in optimistic mood. Frank Dick had forecast 'between twenty-three and twenty-six serious medal chances'. All the big stars were there, two of them defending titles they had won in Athens four years earlier, both against much tougher opposition. Steve Cram had to face Sebastian Coe in the 1500 metres, the man who had beaten him in Los Angeles, and Daley Thompson was to meet his three main rivals in the decathlon – Hingsen, Wentz and Kratschmer – in front of their home crowd.

Optimism must always be tinged with anxiety for it not to become braggartism, and there were enough instances in the past, mainly at Olympic Games where British flames of hope had turned to ashes of despair, for a note of caution to be sounded. Nevertheless, as the team assembled in their headquarters, there was an air of quiet confidence.

This was to be the fourteenth staging of the Championships, which had begun (without British participation) in 1934. The sprint roll of honour contained many famous names – Valeriy Borzov had won four individual titles and the Italian Pietro Mennea had won six medals in all. In the 100 metres Britain's record was dismal – only our steeplechasers in the men's track events had done worse – with just three medals: two bronze with George Ellis in 1954 and Peter Radford four years later, and one gold from the only British sprinter ever to have won the title, Jack Archer, exactly forty years earlier.

The fastest man in Europe was the Russian Viktor Bryzgin, a hundredth of a second faster than Linford. There were nine men that year who had run faster than 10.2 seconds. Emmelmann, the East German, was not there to defend the title he had won in Athens. Of the medallists, only Woronin showed up.

On the evening of 26 August, a short while after the women marathon runners had left the Neckar Stadium, twenty-seven sprinters prepared for the opening round of the 100 metres.

I went to Stuttgart expecting to win. In previous races that season I had beaten a lot of the top contenders, including Woronin and the Frenchman Bruno Marie-Rose. In Britain, though, ever since his selection the media had become very excited about Allan Wells, almost willing him to win, to have the come-back that would make for a fairy-tale ending. After all, there is nothing that the press like more than a good fairy-tale!

This was typified by the television commentaries, which I heard on video when I returned to Britain. Allan was in the first heat, again wearing his knee-length shorts – this time a pair of cut-down Nike tights. He won in 10.31 seconds, a season's best. As each heat unravelled, so his time remained the fastest and the commentators became more and more excited. I ran in the fifth and final heat and won easily in 10.25 seconds, hardly evoking any comment over the air-waves.

Mike McFarlane also qualified and went forward to the semi-finals. Marian Woronin pulled up after thirty metres of his heat with a torn leg muscle, so he was out of the Championships.

The first semi-final the next evening (almost all the events were held at night) saw Bringmann, Bryzgin, Marie-Rose and Wells all together. The East German won, the Frenchman came second and Allan qualified in third place. I won my semi comfortably in 10.19 seconds, just a fraction slower than Bringmann and Marie-Rose. Mac came in fifth but with the same time as Richard, the Frenchman, and after a British protest he was allowed to go forward as the track had a nine-lane straight. It was good to see him there and to have three British sprinters in a European final.

An hour and a half later we lined up. I was relaxed, confident, with just the right amount of adrenalin pumping through my veins. 'Don't let anybody beat you, don't come back without the gold,' my friends had said to me, and I was determined not to let them down. A lot of people, including many members of the press, thought that Allan was going to win, were almost praying that he was going to win. They still thought he was the top British sprinter. But I knew they were living in the past, knew too that there was no way that Allan Wells was going to beat me. I was in lane 3; next to me, in 4, was Bringmann, then Marie-Rose and Allan Wells. The crowd fell silent as the starter called us to our blocks. The stadium was bathed in floodlights. I looked down towards the end of the straight. In ten seconds or so I would be either triumphant or in sackcloth and ashes.

Allan got away to the best start and led for the opening thirty metres (the commentators were going berserk!). I joined the leaders at the half-way mark and then powered my way to the front, crossing the line, half a metre up, in 10.15 seconds, a new Championship record.

I felt pleased of course, but strangely enough I didn't feel as elated as perhaps I should have done: not as elated as I had been after setting my British record in Madrid. Maybe you need an element of surprise to feel like that, and I had believed, felt deep down inside, that I was going to win this title.

The crowd had enjoyed the race – they always appreciate it more when somebody comes through to win as I had done. A British supporter thrust a Union Jack into my hand and I set off on my lap of honour, the first British sprinter to win the title in forty years, the first black man ever to win it. I stood on the winner's rostrum swathed in the Union Jack, the photographers' lightbulbs flashing, the crowd clapping, cheering, other Union Jacks being waved from side to side. They played 'God Save the Queen'. It was a great, great moment.

Later Sir Arthur Gold, then President of the European Athletic Association, wrote a letter to the British team management reprimanding me for wearing the flag on the rostrum and covering my tracksuit. I had felt proud to be British that night; the crowd could see that pride etched on my face in the picture on the stadium scoreboard. The British team, perhaps, was inspired by our first gold medal, and at home millions of people went to bed happy. The only people (or so I thought) who were miffed were the council members of the European Athletic Association, steeped in their protocol. I thought it was uncalled for.

In fact, there was another group who were not happy and who

expressed their unhappiness in no uncertain terms to me on my return. Many people in the black community, people that I had thought of as friends, said to me that I should not have worn the flag that night. There was a feeling that by doing so I was siding with the white community, not showing solidarity with my own people. They always ended, 'And you're not even British!' I told them that I was British, that I had gone to Stuttgart under the British flag. I had left Jamaica when I was seven years of age and had lived in England for nineteen years. I'm more British than Jamaican. I explained that I had felt that it was the right thing to do; it expressed what I felt. I would do it again.

In the race Steffen Bringmann had won the silver and Bruno Marie-Rose the bronze. Allan came in fifth, with Mac just behind him.

At the press conference afterwards the press were still obsessed with Allan. I paid him a tribute, saying, 'He's the godfather of British sprinting . . . he has shown us that we can take on the Americans and beat them. It's a pity how it has turned out for him, but that's the way it goes.'

He acted strangely towards me in Stuttgart. I was talking to Mike McFarlane when Allan came up and interrupted us and spoke to Mac, looking me over but not saying anything to me. Yet I had met Margot and Allan in 1984 and had got on well with them. I thought that he lacked confidence, that for a person who had achieved what he had the composure wasn't there. Allan should, I feel, have been more ambassadorial for the sport. He should have raced a lot more, beaten a lot more people; he was certainly capable of it. Perhaps it was because the Americans had not been at the Moscow Olympics that he wasn't sure of himself; yet he had beaten them later. It seemed to me that he needed reassurance, needed people other than Margot to believe in him. He wasn't strong enough to boost his own confidence. A tragedy in a way, for I thought that Allan Wells had been a great athlete.

A big disappointment for me was the fact that Ron wasn't there. For him to go to Stuttgart he would have had to pay his own way (I was gaining only a pittance from athletics at this time). I thought this was unfair, and I'm very glad that since then the system has changed. Allan had Margot, his coach, in the village, and I thought that medal hopes should all have had their coaches with them. I telephoned Ron and he was, of course, absolutely delighted. I was happy in that I felt that I had paid him back a little for the thousands of hours he had spent at West London Stadium, stopwatch in hand, urging us all on to greater things.

The next evening, the Thursday, I was brought back down to earth with a bump. I had qualified in the heats of the 200 metres that morning quite comfortably with 20.78 seconds. Allan, too, had qualified but poor Todd Bennett pulled a hamstring in the home straight and literally leapt out of the Championships. In the semi-final, however, I felt nothing. There was no essential adrenalin flowing; I didn't feel excited. I ran sluggishly and on the line I was caught by the East German Olaf Prenzler, the defending champion, shunted back to fifth place and out of the final.

The previous night I had got carried away, talking at length to the press and television when I should have been back in our quarters calming down, relaxing and getting some sleep. This is where good team management would have helped. I think they should have been more protective. Even so, I did feel an enormous sense of anti-climax in the 200 metres heats and semi-finals; I had not been through this in the Common-wealth Games because of my injury, and my lack of experi-ence showed. Allan did qualify, and ran well for fifth in the final.

All that was left was the relay, with heats on the Saturday, the penultimate day of the Championships. Our team picked itself: the Scotsman Elliott Bunney, Daley Thompson, Mike McFarlane, and me on the anchor leg. In the preliminaries only one team was to be eliminated. We came second to France in our heat, qualifying easily. As it turned out, the team to be knocked out was the West German team in heat two. They messed up a baton change and failed to finish, creeping from the track with the ribald comments of the crowd in their ears!

In Sunday's final we were drawn in the outside lane. I could view the progress of the race from where I was standing, just before the home straight, and I could see that Elliott and Daley had kept us in the hunt. I prepared myself for the baton change as Mac set off on his leg, so I did not see what happened there. Mel Watman wrote in *Athletics Weekly*:

Now in any circumstances Mike McFarlane runs a good bend and usually a great one: but what Vladimir Muravyev unleashed on the third leg left everybody gasping! It's very easy to exaggerate in athletics, and five metres can become ten without much bother; however, by the time Viktor Bryzgin got away on the anchor nobody doubted he was on his way to Soviet gold. In second place Frank Emmelmann had to be at his very best as Linford Christie charged home for the British team, pushed all the way by Bruno Marie-Rose and Stefano Tilli, but the East German held on well as Linford was given the fastest 'anchor' split of 9.1.

Bryzgin at the press conference said, 'It was easy for me because the others had achieved a wide margin so that I felt sure.'

We gained the bronze medal. What happened in the relay at the European Championships bears an important relationship to some of the friction, argument and unpleasantness that occurred, mostly between Frank Dick and me, over the following two years, so it is important to record an unbiased, respected outsider's view of what actually took place.

My 100 metres win had set the team off to a great Championships. It seems to work that way. An early success can boost morale, give confidence. I think a lot of the team said, 'Well, if Linford can do it, I can do it!' That is the effect it can have. I always tell the younger athletes to go out and do it, to believe in themselves. When you've made the final, you're as good as anyone there. There are two main ingredients: determination and belief.

It was, in medal terms, Great Britain's greatest ever European Championships. Day after day gold medals were captured. On the Thursday, on a cool, damp evening, Sebastian Coe took his first major 800 metres title, followed home by Tom McKean and Steve Cram. On the Friday Daley Thompson successfully beat off the German challenge and retained his decathlon crown, and Roger Black, just twenty years of age, added not only a European title to his Commonwealth gold but a new British record as well. Fatima Whitbread gained victory in the javelin, and the tears of Edinburgh were turned into laughter and bum-wiggling for the television cameras. The previous day she had set a new world record in the preliminaries. On the final day, in warm sunshine, Cram held off Coe to win again, and Jack Buckner, with an enormously courageous run, took the gold medal in the 5000 metres.

The final event of the meeting was the 4 × 400 metres relay. It was an electrifying race, made more so as the runners approached the third stage. Here, Brian Whittle, in his first major championships, awaited Kriss Akabussi. In the mêlée that is a 1600 metres relay change-over area, Akabussi trod on Whittle's heel, dislodging his spike. Undaunted, the young Scot chased after the opposition in one shoe and came in with them to the final take-over. The rest, as they say, is history, as Roger Black brought Britain home for their eighth gold medal. If anyone had doubted that the gods had been smiling on British athletics that August week in Stuttgart, the final event must have convinced them.

My family were absolutely delighted when I returned. Dad said to me, 'Just imagine if you had packed it in when I told you to! It was a test, you know, a test to see if you were determined enough.' I could tell he was very proud. At the club, at the track, everyone was full of congratulations. I was voted Club Athlete of the Year.

On the evening of 29 December 1976, just five months after his double silver medal success at 800 and 1500 metres in the Montreal Olympics, twenty-two-year-old Ivo van Damme died in a car crash on Belgium's autoroute A7 near the town of Orange. It was a tragic ending to what could have, undoubtedly would have, been a golden career. His death spawned one of the great Grand Prix meetings of Europe, the Ivo van Damme Memorial Meeting, held annually in the Heysel Stadium in Brussels, itself a scene of appalling tragedy just over a year earlier at football's European Cup Final.

This year, 1986, the world's greatest distance runners were in action: Said Aouita just missed a world record in the 2000 metres, and Steve Cram set a meeting record of 3 minutes 30.15 seconds. The Belgian William van Dijck sent the large crowd into ecstacy with a new national record in the steeplechase. In the 100 metres was Ben Johnson, who had run under 10.10 seconds no less than nine times that season, a record for the era of electrical timing. He was to face Linford in their first clash since the Commonwealth Games.

I like the Ivo van Damme with its powerful floodlights and big, enthusiastic crowd. It is the only major meeting that the Belgians stage regularly, and they make the most of it. Wilfred Meert, the promoter, puts us all in the Sheraton Hotel and looks after us well. Ben was after his tenth clocking under 10.10 in one season, achieving it with 10.06 seconds. He was delighted, because Carl Lewis had managed only seven! I was pleased at being only a metre behind which I had lost at the start, but it was all really anti-climactic after Stuttgart.

We flew home, getting to our hotel at around 3 a.m. and then straight out the next day for the final event of the British season, the McVitie Challenge at Crystal Palace. In the 100 metres Allan got away to a fine start, I came through fast at the end, there was a photo-finish between us and he got the verdict. After he had crossed the line he did a somersault in celebration. His time was 10.31 seconds; I was two-hundredths behind. He was happy.

It was time to take a few weeks off – no more – but that allowed time for reflection on the year. If I had written the script myself it could not have turned out better: two European titles and a British record. I naturally felt very good about it and proud of myself for the discipline I had shown during the winter in getting down to the work necessary to achieve the successes I had obtained. I felt good inside, too, because I had been able, in some tangible way, to thank Ron, my girlfriend and my parents for all their help and support. I had gone through the most difficult period in an athlete's career, that time before he makes the breakthrough, when he has difficulty in finding the right kind of competition, when money is tight. I had managed it and had had a golden Stuttgart.

I enjoyed the congratulations and little bit of adulation, but I managed to keep some words of my father's in my mind. When he saw on television the public cheering me and reaching out to shake my hand, he said, 'You know, it's not everyone who says "well done" to you that means it. And it's not everyone who comes to a meeting who wants to see you win. Keep it all in perspective.'

I hope that I do. I was still very pleased, however, when the statistician Ian Hodge told me at the end of the year that I had moved from being 156th in the world 100 metres ranking list in 1985 to 4th in 1986! Now I had to start thinking in world terms, for those Championships were coming in 1987.

9
Roads to Rome

Another winter, another show to plan for: weeks of weight training, heavy tyre pulling, track sessions, working and refining, followed by warm-weather training at Lanzarote. No one can say that athletes aren't creatures of habit! I won the Indoor Championships 200 metres, beating John Regis, who in the following month beat Ade Mafe's record in Budapest during a match against Hungary, with 20.85 seconds. He was obviously coming into form.

I travelled back to Athens, partly in order to make up for my ignominious run in the European Indoor there in 1985. I won the 200 metres in fine style, clocking my best indoor time of 21.05 seconds. I felt that there was more to come, and looked forward to running against John Regis in the European Indoor Championships in Lievin three weeks later. I was well satisfied; I had beaten what I considered to be a bogey track for me, determined not to let either the track or the stadium get the better of me.

I had experienced a similar feeling of determination in the past. Just after I had passed my driving test I drove up a local hill on the way to my aunt's house, coming to traffic at a standstill. I couldn't hold the car on the clutch and I rolled back down the hill, getting very embarrassed, especially when a man had to help me push the car up the hill again! I promised myself there and then that I was going to master that hill if it killed me, and every day afterwards I went there and drove up it, holding the car on the clutch, until I was successful. To me it was a great personal achievement.

In Athens, where I was competing alongside Nigel Walker and Lesley-Ann Skeet, two of our best hurdlers, I noticed some spots appearing here and there on my body, but as they didn't bother me, I ignored them. After the race they seemed to be coming up a little more, and by the time we arrived back in Britain I was covered in them. Each day they grew in number and I began to get really worried, wondering if, while in Greece, I had caught a contagious disease.

It began to prey on my mind so much that I went to the casualty department of Charing Cross Hospital. They looked me over, said that they didn't know what it was and sent me home. Now I really began to get worried. The spots started appearing on my chest. I decided to go to Hammersmith Hospital, in Du Cane Road, near my training track. I started thinking about AIDS – we were just beginning to hear about it then, though we weren't too sure how you could contract it. I waited there for what seemed ages, and then they put me in a room on my own and told me to put on a paper gown. I thought, in my anxious state, that the orderly gave me a funny look as he left me there. I waited for what, I swear, was another hour before the door opened and in came a man wearing a mask and gloves. I thought, 'Oh, God! This is it! I've caught something really bad. I'm going to die.' The man looked at me in my petrified state. He said, 'Don't worry, it's chicken pox!'

I went home and visited my GP the next day, and he gave me calamine lotion. I discovered spots in places where I didn't think it was possible to get spots. They were on the backs of my hands and even on the soles of my feet. I had spots everywhere. I caught influenza along with the chicken pox. I had to sleep in a tee-shirt, and when all the spots started popping I was in the worst state of my life. I scratched everywhere but my face, and Mandy had to take absence from work to take care of me. When they are sick, men can be the worst! I was in bed for a straight seven days. The spots then started disappearing, so I went training even though they hadn't completely gone. Time was running short for Lievin. I did some light work and felt fine.

The stadium at Lievin was a fine, new one, though in a remote spot not far from Lille in northern France. On my arrival I had another tiff with Frank Dick. He told me that with chicken pox I shouldn't be with the team, and he kept making remarks which made me feel embarrassed. I didn't think it was the sort of behaviour one should expect from a Director of Coaching.

I lined up in my heat of the 200 metres in a favourite indoor lane, the outside one. I was running well until I felt a twinge in my hamstring and pulled up short of the finish line. Although I was feeling well I was obviously weak. The injury put me out of the World Indoor Championships to be staged in March in Indianapolis.

The track at Lievin was fast. Woronin won the 60 metres in a new European record of 6.51 seconds and Bruno Marie-Rose won the 200 metres in 20.36 seconds, a new world record. John Regis set a new British record with 20.54 seconds. I was obviously disappointed not to be taking part in all the action. The British team did well, winning six medals; Colin Jackson took the silver in the 60 metres hurdles, and Todd Bennett won the 400 metres.

We flew back to Heathrow; it had not been a happy trip for me, full of niggling and snide remarks. At the airport Mike Turner, the team manager, came up and asked, 'What is the problem between you and Frank?' I explained my side of the story. I said, 'It's clear that Frank and I can't work together, so obviously he should leave me alone. I don't bother Frank, and I don't think that he should bother me. Apart from team matters I don't think we should have anything to do with each other.'

I didn't get any satisfactory answer from Mike Turner. A stronger team manager would have dealt quickly with what was obviously becoming an increasingly aggravating situation.

I flew immediately to Norway to receive treatment on my hamstring, and didn't run again until the outdoor season. It had not been an auspicious start to the year.

Prague was the venue for the European Cup in June. Britain had always performed well in this competition and we had a strong team once again. In addition to Linford there were most of the British track stars from Stuttgart the year before – Steve Cram, Tom McKean, Roger Black, Tim Hutchings, Colin Jackson, Kirsty Wade, Yvonne Murray. Held over two days, each country entering one athlete per event, it is a competition well suited to the need to keep Britain established as the third-strongest athletic nation in Europe and the fourth in the world.

The weather was warm, the team hotel (not surprisingly perhaps) sparse, the food bearable. Keen Czechoslovakian athletics aficionados haunted the lobby. Currency exchange negotiations for everyone on the 'open' market were conducted between the team's administrator, *John Brown*, and the hotel's elderly porter in a lift that went constantly up and down to the top floor until they were concluded.

Linford was running both the 100 metres and 200 metres, aiming for a sprint double that only one man had previously achieved, the East German Eugene Ray, ten years earlier.

For the press the facilities were as basic as they were at the hotel. Interviews were conducted either against a whitewashed wall at the back of the media area or down a narrow corridor. You needed both good hearing and a strong voice. In the beginning it was agreed that any British athlete in the top four would come forward for interview. As the weekend progressed, that was quickly reduced to first three, first two and then winners only. It was one of our very best team performances.

I won both the 100 and the 200 metres and achieved a great deal of satisfaction from the double. No British athlete had ever done that before, not even Allan, whose best was a gold and a silver. I had again beaten the top sprinters of Europe, firmly establishing myself as the continent's number one. I believed that with that double victory I had now achieved more than most in British athletics, with the exceptions of course, of Coe, Cram and Ovett.

It was an excellent meeting for us on the track. No British male track athlete apart from Jon Solly in the 10,000 metres was placed outside the top three. In the field events it was very different, hardly anybody scoring in the top four. If our field athletes could have performed as well as the track men, we could have won the European Cup.

We'd spent a couple of days practising the relay. Frank changed the order on the day. I believed that I should again have been running the anchor leg, but our Director of Coaching decided otherwise. I felt that he thought I wanted to run the last leg for the glory. I wanted to run it because I thought it was the only way we stood a chance. I was to run second to a young newcomer on the team, David Kirton. Frank wanted David to give me a down-sweep with the baton, but as anyone can observe, when I am in full flight I'm really running high, and this presented David with a problem as he is quite a short fellow. It did not augur well.

True to form we were disqualified at the first change-over

between David and me. He received a lot of criticism, but I thought it was unfair as he was completely new to the team, so I took my share of the blame. It added to our dismal record in the sprint relay in the European Cup. Only once in the last ten years, in 1983, have we been placed in the first three. Yet our 4 × 400 metres relay teams have had considerable success. Something is wrong somewhere.

After the fiasco in Prague I began to wonder whether there was any point in my running in any more relay teams, began to think that it was just a waste of everyone's time. Looking back I suppose it was then that I started to brood about a problem that grew and grew until it burst out into the open at the World Championships.

Trying to look at the subject rationally, I think it was a difference between theory and practice. You have to balance the psychological importance of having your fastest man on the final anchor leg against the theoretical speed of the baton round the track. Frank Dick is one of the most academically knowledgeable coaches in the world, and aside from the personal differences between us, I think he genuinely believed that I was more useful in one of the central legs of the race. If, however, you look at the anchor men in the European Championships in Stuttgart – men such as Bryzgin, Emmelmann, Marie-Rose, Tilli and Kovacs – you will see that they are the fastest in their countries. Our basic problem was that there was no way that we could all sit down with Frank and talk about it. There was no discussion, period. Yet the essential point of relay racing is that it is a team effort.

Prague was the last stadium where I wore conventional running shorts. In 1986 I noticed that the Americans and Italians were wearing extremely skintight shorts, and while there was no chance I was going to wear those, they did set my imagination in motion. Then Allan appeared at Gateshead in those black cycling shorts which reached down to just above his knee. I thought: here is a new fashion trend, and Linford, if you want to be in the swing, you had better give some thought to it. There was some practicality to the new gear as well. Often, after the starter has told you to strip off, you are kept hanging around, mostly for television, and under those circumstances your hamstrings become very vulnerable.

I thought that I would start my own trend, an all-in-one suit. I remembered that Valerie Briscoe-Hooks had her vests pinned to her shorts, which I had thought looked quite smart. So I went to a designer, Denise Vaughan of Deni Vee, and she made me a couple of suits which really pleased me and I believed that I was on to something. I decided to have the suit right down to the knee.

The first time I appeared in the outfit I was ribbed mercilessly. 'How can you possibly wear that?' the other sprinters shouted. But I ran in it and it felt fine. So then I moved to brighter colours. In Madrid I tried an all-white outfit which seemed okay to me. Certainly, I never imagined that it would in any way be see-through. Colin Jackson, with whom I was fairly close by now, was watching the meeting with some athletes on warm-weather training in Portugal. When he next caught up with me there was a wide grin on his face. 'Linford,' he said, in his fine, lilting Welsh accent, 'I saw you on television running in that jazzy white number in Spain. Unless you want to get arrested at the finish, don't ever wear it again.' So I abandoned the 'jazzy white number' and tried hard not to think about the comments of the other athletes who had watched the race with Colin in Portugal.

I lined up for the 100 metres at the AAA Championships and, lo and behold, everybody came out in similar outfits! I had set a fashion but now I had to keep ahead of it, had to keep people wondering what I would wear next. I believe that it enlivened the sport for public and athletes alike. It was and is part of the entertainment. The moment the top stars of track and field stop thinking of themselves as entertainers, then the sport is dead.

My outfits got brighter, more garish. I moved to a yellow and tartan design. Then I got an all-in-one body-length outfit zipped up to the neck – Flo-Jo wore something similar in Rome. However, I decided to dispense with the hood; I didn't see the point of hiding my face. The suit felt fine, quite aero-dynamic. There has also, of course, got to be a practical value to the designs, and in Britain that practical value is keeping warm. The outfits are also useful for training; when I am on the back straight at West London, Ron can see what I'm doing quite clearly, especially on the video afterwards. There is no way that I could skive a session, even if I wanted to, wearing my yellow and tartan suit!

Of course, timing is all-important when embarking on such a programme. You have to do it when you are winning! The other factor that comes into play is size. I believe that you have to be tall to wear the kind of outfits that I do. If, like some sprinters, you are short and stocky and decide to wear the really skintight, knee-length shorts, it can be somewhat indecent. I always tell such guys to try to look at themselves from behind!

In Olympic year there was some fuss made by the Women's AAA about my outfit. It was the first time that the men's and women's championships had been combined and I think that Marea Hartmann, the Secretary, was trying to drum up publicity for her side of the event. She said that some of her council members were worried about the effect my outfit would have on the young girl athletes who were running at the meeting. But I don't think Marea was too serious about this. Certainly she presented me with my medal for the 100 metres and as I stood on the plinth she did not bat an eyelid.

I next ran at Oslo where I set a personal best for 200 metres, so that was encouraging. Then Mike McFarlane and I went to the Nepstadion in Budapest. It was warm and the track is fast. Mac and I were both entered in the 100 metres. There was a strong American squad there, including Lee Macrae and Emmit King, with Ray Stewart Jamaica. I won in 10.03 seconds, a new British record. It was more than compensation for my not having annexed the all-comers record earlier at Portsmouth because of a stronger than allowable following wind. The behaviour of the Americans in the Hungarian capital was ridiculous. They were spreading rumours that Mac and I knew the starter and that I had got away with a false start. It was all nonsense, of course.

So the season continued and the World Championships in Rome began more and more to occupy my mind. Increasingly intruding into those thoughts, though, was the composition of the relay team. We had abortive relay practices. At Gateshead Frank informed me that I was going to run in the B relay team at the meeting, and I refused. Apart from my own pride, what on earth would the public think about seeing the European champion and double sprint winner at the European Cup running in the reserve relay team? The press would have had a field day, and what Frank didn't realize is that he himself would have been a laughing stock. The team management intervened, I ran in the A team and everybody's pride and position were salvaged. It didn't, however, improve the situation between Frank and me.

The World Championships crept gradually nearer, and as they did so the relay running order began to get to me. It was foolish, even stupid; it wasn't as if we were even contenders for a medal. My whole thinking, every waking moment should have been concentrating on the 100 metres in which I was still convinced, despite losing to Carl in Madrid earlier in the season, that I could take the gold medal. Instead I was getting myself into an increasingly confrontational situation, a battle of wills, with the Director of Coaching.

The final meeting before the team left for Rome was at Crystal Palace. After my race I climbed the steps to the press interview room. Answering questions, I told the press the situation as I saw it. I said that unless I was picked for the final leg I wouldn't run. It was reported in the form of an ultimatum, and made the front page of one or two tabloids. Neither my wins in the European Championships and European Cup nor my two British records had ever made the front page – but the fact that I wouldn't run in a relay team had. It seemed to me to be a crazy world. In that frame of mind, I boarded the Alitalia flight for Rome.

10
Roman Crucible

We were at a track well away from the hotel that the Italians had euphemistically dubbed the Athletes' Village, and well away from the training track that was adjacent to the Olympic Stadium. It perplexed us that we were in such a remote spot. Frank Dick said, 'You're running first leg. Lump it or leave it.' These were the first words spoken between us since we had arrived in Rome four days earlier. Nobody had mentioned relays up until then. It seemed like a huge sword of Damocles hanging over the sprinters' heads. I said, 'I'll leave it.'

I had told Ron, who was with me in Rome, that I hadn't seen the point in attending the practice, but he had persuaded me that I ought to attend. John Regis tried to say something, but Frank cut him short. 'I'll decide the team,' he said.

'Frank,' I said, 'if we don't agree on the running order then surely it is something we should sit down and discuss as a team.'

'Don't you want to run?' Frank asked.

I called him an idiot. He told me to leave the track. The exchanges were becoming quite heated. I was getting more and more angry.

Suddenly I saw a whole host of photographers hiding behind the bushes. When I had first arrived I had seen a couple of press people milling around, but now there seemed to be a whole platoon of them, cameras at the ready. One of the photographers was Monty Fresco of the *Daily Mirror*, and seeing him there increased my anger threefold. He had asked me for a photograph of myself when I was young and I had told him to go around and get it from Mandy. He went to her workplace and badgered and finally photographed her, infringing our private lives. Now the photographers all came out and started taking pictures of Frank and me arguing. I believed this to be a private row, and became even more incensed. I kept asking myself how the photographers had arrived there at this particular track.

I walked away from Frank, saying, 'So this is the gratitude you get for running your heart out for Britain.'

My language became worse. I then walked across to the photographers and lost my temper, lost my head. I thought that I had been set up. I was as angry as hell. I raved at them, swore at them, gesticulated at them. They just kept clicking away with their cameras. Finally, my temper spent, I stalked away. The next day, back in Britain, the pictures, some of them quite unedifying, appeared in the newspapers, a number on the front pages.

The situation had not been helped by the fact that the subject of the Stuttgart relay had come up. Frank had accused me before of 'messing up' the relay, and had told me that the rest of the team were of the same opinion. I had told him to look at a video of the race and he would see that it was through my efforts that we had won the bronze. Now, in Rome, Frank turned to Mac and reminded him, in front of me, that he had said I was responsible for messing up the change-over. We were all in a bad temper, acting like children. If I had possessed a gun that day I would have shot Frank; that is how bad I felt.

When I reflected on all this later I knew that I just should not have lost my temper. I should have kept cool. I deeply regret what happened that morning in Rome. I let myself down and I let my sport down. I was just so frustrated by what I thought was Frank's intransigence. It was that, initially, that made me so mad. But it never should have happened. This row, this argument had been brewing all season long. The team manager was well aware of it, knew that it was coming to a head, but took no action. It needed a strong third party to intercede between Frank and me; such a person was not available.

Allan Wells spoke out on the relay issue. He said, 'We've been through all this before and it's about time they were getting things right. I have great sympathy with Linford; what they are doing to him is totally disgraceful.' That was good of him. He and I had had a heart to heart in the hotel following some comments supposedly made by him about me in the press, more particularly in the *Sun*. He was angry about the comments, denied making them and I accepted what he said.

I just couldn't wait to get on with the athletics.

The days leading up to a major championship meeting are always very tense, very difficult, and the second World Championship in Rome was no exception. The Italian capital was experiencing, even by its own standards, a heatwave, and the two hotels that were provided by the authorities as the Athletes' Village were of a mediocre calibre. Add to that the tensions of the coming competition and the situation becomes volatile in no time.

The media were also tense. Out in force a week or so prior to the start of the meeting, they hunted for stories like lions seeking water on a drought-ridden veldt, lingering outside the security fences and eyeing the carabinieri, who would let none through without the appropriate pass. Back home, impatient sports editors waited for them to file as they drank the Latium hills dry of Chianti.

The Stadio Olimpico, a stone's throw from the Tiber, is built on gladiatorial lines. Any self-respecting Christian arriving on a time-warp would immediately feel at home. Alongside it the Marble Stadium, with its tall, marble statues towering above it, served as the warm-up track. It had staged the 1960 Olympic Games when the German Armin Hary, said to be the fastest starter ever, won the 100 metres and the Italians celebrated as their hero Livio Berutti took the 200 metres gold. Allan Wells had won the 1981 World Cup 100 metres here, fully vindicating his Olympic win of the previous year. Wells was back again with the British team, but only just. He failed, through injury, to make the start line.

An intense rivalry was to be renewed between Carl Lewis and Ben Johnson in the short sprint. Lewis – some called him 'The Lip' – was defending the title he had won in Helsinki in 1983; Johnson had first beaten him in 1985 and of their last five encounters he had won four. Verbal exchanges in the days leading up to the opening ceremony had served only to heighten the interest in the event. Others were in contention. Linford, despite his shenanigans, was quietly confident; Ray Stewart had been improving in recent weeks, as had the fast-starting American Lee Macrae. It really was going to be quite a race.

I don't agree with the theory that my becoming emotionally

charged up by the relay affair affected my running in the 100 metres. It would be an easy excuse for me to concur, but my running throughout the preliminary rounds and semi-final really indicated that this was not the case. I hadn't run against Ben that year and I was confident of beating Carl and him, because of the way I had been running. I was improving each year – my 10.03 seconds in Budapest had shown that. I always feel that I am as good as anyone else. I think it is essential to feel that if you are to be a successful athlete.

The first two rounds were on the first day of the Championships, and I cruised them comfortably. In the first round I eased in third behind Pavoni and Bryzgin. Mac also qualified behind a fast Ray Stewart. Allan had scratched, annoying the team management by informing ITN of the fact before he informed them. Carl Lewis, in the seventh heat, ran a championship record of 10.04 seconds and was, I supposed, trying to send a message to Ben.

I drew Lewis in the second round and came in second behind him. I always run just as fast I have to, and as I neared the finish I looked across to make sure that I had qualified, and there was Carl. Some of the press read into that that I was trying to stare him out! Mac again proceeded forward, this time to the semi-final.

The semi-final on the Sunday saw me in Ben's heat and again it was easy qualifying, with Ben first, me second, and third, to the crowd's wild enthusiasm, Pavoni. In the second race Carl came home in 10.03 seconds for yet another Championship best. Ray Stewart was having an excellent meeting and clocked 10.12 for the third-fastest time of the event so far, after Carl's two runs. Mac came seventh in that race, but I thought that he had done well.

I withdrew to our massage parlour, which was in a room like a cave under the concrete seating of the Marble Stadium. After that I listened to my Walkman, and later talked to Ron. It was good to have him in Rome in a major supporting role. I jogged around with Ben well before I started on the important phase of my warm-up. There are not many athletes with whom I will warm-up, but Ben is one of them. He doesn't take rivalry with him off the competitive track, and at that time I considered him to be the Master with myself as the apprentice. Ben said that he'd heard I'd been having some problems and asked what they were.

I explained what had been going on. 'Don't worry about it,' Ben said. 'Let's go out there together and beat Lewis!' I thought that was a very diplomatic way of putting it. We went our separate ways, both recognizing that we had to psych ourselves up for the race.

They called us out into the stadium too early and it was hot, very hot. I was in lane 1, which I found strange considering the positions and times I had achieved in the semi-final. Pavoni, the Italian and overwhelming favourite of the naturally biased crowd, had a good draw. I was next to Lee Macrae, accredited with being one of the world's fastest starters, and I had already decided on my tactics. My start was not at its best in 1987, so I thought, well okay, if I can follow Macrae out then I will be all right.

The adrenalin was pumping away, but as the marksmen made no attempt to tell us to strip off and the minutes dragged by, so it began to ease away. Finally we were called up, the gun fired and on this day Lee Macrae decided to have a bad start! I thought that as I was up with him, I was up with the leaders. I was running blind, but then Macrae faded from view and from my senses. I didn't have a clue what was happening. Ten metres from the line I saw Ray, twisted to dip and strained my hamstring. I thought that I had finished third, but when I studied the television slow-motion replay on the stadium scoreboard I could see that in fact Ray had won the bronze medal.

When I saw Ben's winning time of 9.83 seconds I was totally amazed. I had never thought that anybody could run that fast. It was quite phenomenal and I felt that I had been privileged to run in such a race. In 1989 in a television piece, Daley Thompson picked Ben's run as one of the six greatest performances of all time, and I have to agree with that. I must be honest and say that I don't think I'll ever run that fast. I'm not saying that I won't win World and Olympic titles, just that, at this time, I cannot conceive of myself achieving that time.

I had not run well; I had not done myself justice. My time was slow (10.14), but on the other hand I had run fourth in my first World Championship. I had mixed feelings.

It was the race that ended the pre-eminence of the distance runners in world track and field, almost the end of an era. In British athletics, too, the winds of change were beginning to blow. It was the first time that Coe, Cram and Ovett had not been among the medal winners at a major championship meeting since 1976.

The pre-race hype between Lewis and Johnson had been unprecedented. Johnson's coach, Charlie Francis, an ex-international sprinter himself, had forecast that in perfect conditions Ben would run 9.85 seconds. Lewis contented himself with saying that it was the race that would decide who was the best. 'I felt that Ben panicked in our race in Seville,' Carl said, 'and if someone is with him at sixty metres then I think he is vulnerable.' But there was the rub, for Ben had, according to many, the most explosive start ever in athletics' history and being with him at the three-fifths point in the race was, apparently, beyond the powers of the sprinters gathered in the Stadio Olimpico on this hot August day, Lewis included.

As the eight finalists finally got to their marks, the anticipation was high in the stadium, the tension heavy. Johnson exploded off his starting blocks with more than his usual ferocity, and by ten metres there was daylight between him and the remaining seven. By half-way he was two metres up on the defending champion, and Lewis must have known that his title was speeding away from him. The American narrowed the gap over the closing metres but to no avail, for Ben Johnson was making world history this day with a phenomenal new world record. Lewis, a metre behind, equalled the old world record of 9.93 seconds but could not even console himself with a new American best for he only equalled the time of Calvin Smith. Calvin had set his time at altitude, always beneficial in the 'explosive' events, and indeed the previous record of 9.95 seconds by another American, Jim Hines, had also been set high up in Mexico City. Johnson's had been one of the greatest track and field performances of all time.

'This record is one of the best ever,' Ben said, 'on a par with Bob Beamon. If anyone is going to break it they are going to have to be better than me over the first fifty metres, so it's going to be difficult. Next year I think I can run even faster.' For Lewis it was a sobering experience to lose at major international level, following his Helsinki and Los Angeles exploits.

Ray Stewart of Jamaica had run the race of his life and the time of his life to win the bronze medal. It was the only time he defeated Linford all year. Don Quarrie coached Stewart, and in one of the buses that returned the athletes to the Village at the end of the day's events, as the escorting police motor cyclists' sirens whined and the blue lights flashed and Italian families paused in their evening perambulations to catch a glimpse of these new gladiators, he said simply

*of the greatest 100 metres ever run, 'Lewis was ready, but Ben was
more ready. Ben came here to win.'*

*Of the first four in the race, three had been born in Jamaica, an
amazing achievement for this tiny Caribbean island.*

As it turned out that was the end of my first World Championship. Despite valiant efforts by our physiotherapists, my hamstring did not recover in time for the 200 metres. They were
battling against the odds because they didn't appear to have
the right equipment. It seemed to me that it would be more
advantageous to spend less on officials and more on medical
supplies. Joan Watt did her best – she's absolutely wonderful
and a very considerate person. Knock on her door at 3 a.m. for
a leg massage and I swear she would get up and do it for you,
though she might swear a little under her breath!

Our relay team was disqualified in the opening round of the 4
× 100 metres relay. The only medal we had ever won at a
major championship since 1978 was the bronze we had gained
at Stuttgart in the European.

Rome ended as it had begun, in some controversy. I was told
by the team management not to make any statements to the media
about the relay incident at the training track, and I stuck by that.
Then I discovered that Frank had given his version, so it seemed to
me that there were two laws in existence. Jim Rosenthal of ITV
kept asking me to give my side of the story and in the end I did,
appreciating the opportunity to put the record straight.

I was miserable in Rome. Normally I am one of the happiest
people in the team. The hotel that we stayed in was just awful,
and the food provided was worse. In my opinion the Italian Feder-
ation should even now refund substantial sums of money to all
the countries that attended for the dreadful food and facilities.
Most of the meals were cold and inedible, but we had to eat
them because we were hungry. One day they handed us some
chipped potatoes, and there was enough oil on them to boil
another portion. A later irony was that in Seoul the Italians took
their own chef!

We were cramped in our hotel rooms and when it rained the
water came in. At the back of the hotel the army suddenly
produced a generator designed to penetrate the deepest slumber
and then added a searchlight which they shone, lighting up not

Above: At Bislet, for one of the great European Grand Prix meetings

Right: At the World Championships in Rome in 1987

Below: The first 'leg' of a great winning sprint double for Great Britain at the European Cup in Prague in 1987

Up against Allan Wells at Crystal Palace in 1987

Talking with Jim Rosenthal of ITV after my European Cup win of 1987. Jim is one of the media's most considerate and kind men

The greatest sprint ever? Ben Johnson beats Carl Lewis at the World Championships in 1987 and sets a world record of 9.83 seconds

My second European Indoor title, the 60 metres in Budapest in 1988 when I set a new British record in the semi-final

A rare defeat by a British athlete. Lincoln Asquith wins the AAA Indoor 60 metres with a brilliant start and gives me a sobering moment

A significant moment in Olympic year at Crystal Palace. I beat Chidi Imo, Africa's fastest man, and then fly to Nice three days later to repeat the win and give myself a big boost for Seoul

only the surrounding countryside in their search for Red Brigade terrorists, but our hotel rooms as well.

Behind the façade, behind the glittering ceremony and the IAAF delegates' hotels which were far superior to those for the athletes, there was a lot of wrong-doing, not least the cheating that went on in the long jump where they tried to wangle a bronze medal for Evangelisti, the Italian, by inaccurate measuring. Although this received some publicity, it did not compare with the media attention given a year or so later to the drug problems in Seoul. Surely cheating is cheating, whatever form it takes, and I do not believe that the 'crimes' committed at the Olympics were any worse than that committed in Rome. Yet the former were magnified a hundredfold in terms of publicity.

I took a little time off in Rome to do some shopping. Many people imagine that it is a glamorous life, jetting around the world for the big athletics meetings and receiving much media attention. While I will grant you that it beats filing for the Inland Revenue, it is a suitcase existence and no matter how glamorous the location of the meeting we very rarely see beyond the airport, the hotel and the stadium. Because of my injury I did get as far as the Spanish Steps and the shops in Rome, but that was the extent of my sightseeing.

When I reviewed my performance I thought, well, it was my first major World Championship and I came fourth. Ray Stewart is an experienced athlete, coached by the old master Don Quarrie. The field in the final was probably the greatest ever brought together, and it had produced a world record of staggering proportions. One newspaper ran the headline 'Christie's a Chump!' I didn't even know what 'chump' meant and had to go around asking people. I was glad to get back to Britain.

*From the moment that the teams flew into Leonardo da Vinci airport until the moment they left, they were under a cloak of security that was to enshroud the Championships. Kalashnikov-toting guards were everywhere and armed carabinieri escorted teams to and from the Athletes' Village – the hotels Ergife Palace and Princess. Accreditation**

*The procedure of issuing passes to allow athletes and officials access to certain areas of the complex.

was a nightmare. There was the raising of the shoulders, the tilt of the head, the spread of the hands, the look that says 'not possible'.

From the first day of competition onwards there was the complicated process of conquering the logistics of the Stadio Olimpico complex. Which accreditation pass can get you where? What is the quickest way from the warm-up track to the stadium? How to get athletes into the call-up area? How to get air into the physiotherapists' caves beneath the stands?

There was a mixed area near the finish in the stadium where press and athletes were supposed to meet and chat convivially after races. It was a hell on earth, a dark cavern which was a cross between Dante's Inferno and the Wig and Pen. Desperate scribes battled with bureaucracy to try to get to the athletes. Latin temperaments rose in exasperation in direct proportion to their owners' frustration. Arms were waved, people were pushed, blows were very nearly struck. There was a babble of languages and much pointing of fingers. Already overheated athletes boiled some more in this airless pit, changed slowly and tried to creep away. At the end of one evening Francesco Panetta lost an ill-organized 10,000 metres and thousands of Italians mentally threw themselves into the Tiber. It was that sort of week.

The British team did well, but not brilliantly. Only Fatima Whitbread gained a gold medal. The hurdlers Jon Ridgeon and Colin Jackson gained silver and bronze respectively behind the American Greg Foster. At the subsequent press conference held high in the stadium stand, Foster hushed even the most hardened of hacks by dedicating his gold medal to his mother who had died two years earlier, along with other members of his family, in a car crash. The parade of the athletes to these press conferences was like the opening of a Marvin Hagler title fight. There were many gesticulations, much macho shouting, escorts of armed guards – the Italian nation at its most exuberant.

Staying cool and lovely in the midst of this bubbling cauldron was the interpreter Anna Legnani, seemingly word-perfect in a host of languages – including, after Steve Cram's conference, Geordie. She it was who interpreted for various French, German and Italian journalists as John Regis, our sole sprint medallist with a bronze in the 200 metres, told everybody that for one flickering moment he (and many others) had thought he had won gold. 'I smiled for a brief moment in triumph,' he said, 'then, as the photographers moved to

Calvin Smith, I knew I was mistaken. It was my greatest race and a British record.'

Putting Rome behind him Linford returned home, a new target added to his aims: the British 200 metres record.

11
Reflections

I took more time off than usual after the World Championships, feeling that I needed a break. I flew to New York to stay for twelve days with my sister, who lives there. They say that you can easily spot the tourists in the Big Apple – they are the people walking around gazing at the sky, at the tops of the skyscrapers. Well, that was me as I toured Central Park, Statue of Liberty and Empire State Building. I had a relaxed time.

Ron normally allows his athletes two weeks off, so by the time I arrived back at West London Stadium they were well into winter training. I joined them and the going for a week or two was very hard. Ron and I take each year as it comes and we always plan for me to run a personal best every season. I find it difficult to understand those who say they are planning for next year's championships – what is the point, they could be run over by a bus before next year? I leave all the details of training to Ron – he is the expert – and my racing programme is planned between Andy Norman, Ron and me with Andy always playing an important part.

It was in the winter of 1987–88 that I announced I was going to race mostly in Britain in Olympic year. I was fed up with the European promoters who seemed obsessed by the American sprinters. It seemed to me that when the top men from the States came over, the first person to oppose them, to make a good confrontational meeting, should have been the European champion. Having eight men from outside the continent in a race did not seem to me to be good business. The promoters didn't agree.

Sprinting is my living, and I didn't think I was being paid enough to appear in Britain. Andy does his best by us, and overall most get a fair deal.

I believe that I am an entertainer. You get to realize that gradually, as the applause grows. Do people pay to go to athletics meetings because it's 'athletics', or do they go to see the individual stars? It is a question with which promoters and television are constantly grappling, but I believe that the answer is self-evident. As an entertainer I run in bright colours and I run for the public. Their response never ceases to amaze me, as does the accolade accorded to me by the fans. I get fan mail, I even get marriage proposals, and I have to confess that I love it all and appreciate it, too. I always do my best, run my heart out, give one hundred per cent for the athletics fans, and I like to believe that they in turn appreciate that, as well as the fact that I do run a lot in Britain. There is natural resentment when a number of our middle-distance stars spend all their time running abroad.

When, after a race on my lap of honour (when I've won!), I wave and clap at the crowd, blow kisses at them and bow, it is not theatricality but very genuine feeling. It is my way of showing my appreciation for their support, and it comes from the heart. There is no greater way to get the adrenalin flowing at the start of a race than when the commentator builds up to my name, the crowd waiting and then at its announcement bursting into loud cheering. It makes you want to win for them, makes you determined not to let them down.

From this you can see that I am a very emotional person. Sometimes on the rostrum I get a lump in the throat and my eyes well up. Big men don't cry so the saying goes, so I hold back the tears – but they're there none the less.

I spent Christmas with my family that year. I am a family man, and mine has been of great help to me. Without them, Mum and Dad and my brothers and sisters, I would not be where I am today. They were a tremendous help during that period when my athletics earning power was almost nil but I had to devote all my time to athletics to achieve success. Mum and Dad are my greatest fans, but they have never been to a meeting! I am really glad of it; I don't think I would want them to be there, just in case I lost. They would be so disappointed that Dad would feel the necessity to '*have a word*'. My sisters have been along to a couple of events, and Mum and Dad watch my performances on television, as well as videos of my races. Nobody is allowed to utter a word as I am going to my marks. Neighbours and friends tell me that when I am racing you can hear the noise right down the street; it is as if I am running in Dad's front room! I suspect that on the night of the Olympic final all the neighbours were rudely awakened at 4 a.m. I know that many sportsmen have not received this kind of support, so I am all the more grateful for it.

As the winter wore on I did some hard thinking about Rome. I realized that I could have been in deep trouble there: I came close to inflicting a serious injury on Frank Dick. Deep down inside myself I am an easy-going person, but when finally provoked I get very angry indeed. Some people tend to take advantage of a placid nature – that is only human – so I realized that in order to prevent abuse of my personality I would have to put up a barrier to protect my inner self. I also had to let people know where the line of acceptability is drawn.

I indulged in some self-analysis. It was the first time in years that I had blown my top in such a way, and I vowed that it would never happen again, that I would save all my aggression for the track. I also realized that I have a responsibility, not only to young black kids but to all young people, of every colour and creed. The tendency to categorize black sportsmen and women differently from the rest is faintly racist and, I believe, totally unnecessary. I think that perhaps some people are still looking for the Great White Hope, as they did in the days of John L. Sullivan, the first black World Heavyweight boxing champion. I object to being called the 'Black Panther'. Ralph Metcalfe, that great sprinter of the early thirties and adversary of Jesse Owens, was not, I suspect, enamoured of being known as the 'Midnight Express'. In Jamaica the people never referred to DQ (as Don Quarrie is almost universally known) as a black anything. He was just a sprinter, and that is exactly what I consider myself.

Martin Luther King once said, 'I want to be the white man's brother, not his brother-in-law.' That is how I feel. I am running for everybody in Britain, irrespective of colour or creed.

The AAA tried during the winter months to bring an end to the hostility between Frank Dick and me. I met the then Chairman of the AAA, Bill Ferguson, who asked me what the problem was all about. I told him that I didn't really see the point in him talking to Frank and me separately. What was needed was for us to get together with an arbitrator. There were three sides to the story, I said: Frank's version, mine, and the truth.

In the end Frank and I met of our own volition. We discussed our differences and agreed to call an armistice. We came together on one point, and that was our attitude towards the media. It had been an eye-opener to me in 1987 when I realized how naïve I had been about the press, discovered how they believe they have some God-given right to intrude on the privacy of well-known individuals in the name of journalism. Both Frank and I had been telephoned, informed of remarks supposedly made by the other, and asked for our comments. We agreed to contact each other first if that happened in the future, before making a reply.

Frank and I will basically never get along. We are chalk and cheese; our personalities are radically different and likely to abrade each other. We both have very firm views on relay racing which can never be reconciled. It had become obvious a few years back that this was a problem for Britain. It was a problem which the team manager, Mike Turner, should have faced up to very quickly and brought to a conclusion one way or the other. He didn't, and the Rome fracas was the result.

In December a series of articles appeared in *The Times* by two journalists, Pat Butcher and Peter Nichols, on drug abuse in athletics. Basically it was about certain British officials allegedly colluding in drug-test avoidance at some meetings in the early eighties. These allegations were strongly denied by all of them, and writs were later served. In one of these articles one of the reporters wrote that a sprinter had told him that if you are not on drugs, specifically steroids, then it is like racing in plimsolls against every one else in spikes. The inference was obvious, so I immediately telephoned Butcher late one evening.

'I didn't like your article,' I told him. 'I've never taken anything. I'm as clean as a whistle; they can test me any time, anywhere.' He asked if I would say that 'on the record'. I agreed, and next day they sent a photographer along to West London Stadium and I was pictured wearing my 'Pure Talent' tee-shirt with 'No Additives' inscribed on the back. I had to wear it back to front for the photographer. I was the only athlete to speak out, to go on the record. No other international said a word, and the

International Athletes Club made no comment. All the remarks and innuendoes were allowed to pass by.

A few months later the IAC, inspired by Jack Buckner, suddenly produced a paper for all internationals to sign agreeing to be random tested at a moment's notice, anywhere, any time. I refused to sign it, and so did Steve Ovett – we had already made our positions clear on the subject. The IAC held a press conference to trumpet their document and announced that every international athlete had signed it with the exceptions of Steve and me. I think they thought it was a way to gain publicity for their petition. The inference was, of course, that we had something to hide. I was very angry and threatened to resign from the IAC over the issue. They were very naïve, as was proven later in the season when Jeff Gutteridge, the pole vaulter, was found positive after a random test taken at Lanzarote. He had signed the petition. Who, under normal circumstances, wouldn't have? As Angela Issajenko said at the Canadian Drug Abuse Enquiry in 1989, people are never going to admit to taking drugs. They are always going to deny any involvement. My reason for not signing the petition was quite clear: when I had spoken out the previous December not one other international, nor the IAC, had raised a peep when our sport was being vilified. I still have not forgiven Jack or the IAC.

My stand on drug-taking is well known and documented. When I die they can perform an autopsy and they will find that I have never ever taken an illegal substance. I know that if I suddenly start feeling pains anywhere in my body, I don't have to worry that it is the side effects of drugs, as, regrettably, some athletes do. If, say, my left breast becomes enlarged, I do not have to contemplate whether it is a result of taking illegal substances.

Shortly after Rome Carl began speaking out on the drug issue, implicating by suggestion Ben and his coach Charlie Francis. Not much came of it. For years, of course, there have been rumours about this and that athlete. One of the major side effects of taking steroids is a noticeable change in body structure, changes in features. The athletes are often the first to start noticing such changes. If *we* can notice differences in people, then how is it that the IAAF and other governing bodies do not notice them as well and start target-testing them during the winter months? Is there a strong enough will to stamp out drug abuse?

Much of the publicity that drug usage has received over the last two or three years has been counter-productive. In a letter to a newspaper one man commented that he was taking his six-year-old daughter to her school sports day when she asked, 'Daddy, can I have some of the drugs that Ben Johnson took to make me run fast?' She had obviously picked that up from television. As another example, *Athletics Weekly* carried an article with lurid photographs about one of their reporters who had visited a gymnasium where you could obtain drugs, especially steroids. The magazine not only named the drugs but also the dosages that were recommended. To me that was total irresponsibility, especially as the magazine is aimed at a younger readership.

Of course there is drug abuse in athletics, but I do not believe that it is as widespread as the press and some of the anti-campaigners make out. Of course we have cheats in our sport, but there are cheats in every walk of life. As Andy Norman has said, athletics only reflects the society in which it exists. Charlie Francis said at the Canadian Enquiry that all the world's top athletes were on drugs – that was his excuse for encouraging Ben to go on steroids. He had to justify himself somehow, both to himself and to the public. He also said that he would destroy track and field, but fortunately the strength of the sport is greater than any of its parts.

On the other side there are those who would like to perform witch-hunts in order to scare track and field athletes into giving up drugs. This is a fearful path to embark upon, for the world of drug gossip and innuendo is almost as unsavoury as that of drug-taking itself. Athletic careers and whole lives can be threatened simply by suggestion.

No athlete can feel satisfied by a performance achieved with the aid of drugs; natural success lasts much longer. Nor can any athlete look forward to a long and healthy life if they use drugs to aid their performance. Some may even have to countenance death, as did the German heptathlete Birgit Dressel, if they embark on a programme of drug-taking. No success in the world is ever worth that.

During the pre-Olympic winter I trained with Daley Thompson, and I have to record it as both a most exciting and elevating experience. In terms of motivating those around him Daley has no peer, and if when he finally hangs up his spikes they can convince him to go into coaching, he will be sensational. It is difficult for the athletes who know Daley to understand why so many people are unable to get along with him. With us he is relaxed, amusing and always considerate, urging us all to the highest achievements.

He has the ability to get you into the right frame of mind, to get you mentally prepared. In every session that you undertake with him, Daley explains his ideas. He is constantly talking to you about your performance, about how you are reacting, building up your confidence throughout the training session. He is quite brilliant. Sometimes he set the sessions, and they were quite the toughest bouts of training that I have ever undertaken. Throughout the winter, when he was around, he made me work, work, work. Everything I subsequently achieved in 1988 is owed in substantial measure to Daley.

We made our usual visit to Lanzarote in 1988, but the place had changed. There was a new management, who were eager to use top-class athletes for publicity purposes but appeared to want to give nothing in return. They invited the Spanish and local press to watch us train, which is exactly the opposite of what we were hoping for.

I do not train specifically for the indoor season, but continue to carry out my normal programme of track endurance running, tyre-pulling and weight-training. I often wonder what I would be able to achieve if, one year, I did train especially for the indoor meetings, but it would be an error to try that because the indoor is just a side-show to the main events, which are the big outdoor meetings in the summer. But if you set a personal best indoors, on the heavy training that you have been undertaking, it is a tremendous incentive. You go back into concentrated training in the spring highly motivated, starting off from a new plateau. That is the greatest value of indoor competition. It was in that frame of mind that I moved into the Olympic year indoor season, saying, as I had been doing for a long time, 'In '88, I'll graduate!'

12
On Song for Seoul

There was a double focus to my 1988 indoor season: the usual National Championships at Cosford, and the European in Budapest. At Cosford I received a sobering shock, being beaten by Lincoln Asquith in the 60 metres. Lincoln had a 'dream start', and although I was closing and closing I couldn't make it. If the race had been over 62 metres then I felt I would have won, but there are no championships at this distance so I had to be content with second place. I do not want to detract from Lincoln's performance in any way; he is a very talented athlete, but somehow that talent seems to have gone to waste. It was the first time that I had run a 60 metres in years and I improved my personal best to 6.63 seconds, which I was pleased with – but not so happy, obviously, to lose to Lincoln by one-hundredth of a second. I won the 200 metres easily.

In Glasgow the new indoor stadium at Kelvin Hall, with its attractive blue 200 metres track and wide bends, staged a Dairy Crest International against France. There was a highly enthusiastic capacity crowd. I won both the 60 and 200 metres, but it was in the final event, the relay, that I received my greatest fillip. Over the first three legs the French had shown us a clean pair of heels, especially with superior baton-passing. When I took over, Bruno Marie-Rose, the indoor world-record holder, was already away. I gave chase, passed him and brought us home to victory. I was timed at 20.4 seconds. The noise from the crowd was incredible. Frank Dick came rushing over to congratulate me – a sign of the new understanding operating between us! I travelled back to London in high spirits for the big meeting in Hungary.

I raced in Ghent against the Canadian Desai Williams and lost over 60 metres, but I beat the American record holder James Butler at 200 metres with 20.55 seconds, the fastest indoor time in the world that year. In training, Daley was constantly into motivation. 'You'll crush the British record this year,' he said.

'No I won't,' I replied.

'I'll bet you any money you like,' Daley continued, 'that you'll run 6.55 seconds or faster.'

Every time he arrived at West London Stadium for training he kept to this theme, adding that I would win the European Indoor. After a while it became quite infectious.

In Budapest the heats were, as usual, very easy. I knew that a lot depended on my start, which was just not consistent enough. In my memory was Lincoln's wonderful start at Cosford. But I also remembered Daley's words. I was the third fastest at 60 metres on arrival in Hungary, behind a young East German, Sven Matthes, and the experienced Belgian Ronald Desruelles. I won my semi-final in fine style, fulfilling Daley's prophecy and setting a new British record of 6.55 seconds. It was a peculiar race. Afterwards they told me that I had had the fastest reaction off the blocks, that by ten metres I was down and by fifty metres I was leading by two metres. Clearly my pick-up needed attention. Half of Daley's forecast had come true – but would the rest?

In the final I had a worse start than in the semi but I came through strongly to take the title in a slightly slower time of 6.57 seconds. I was pleased; it showed that I was sprinting nearer to the very best. In the 200 metres I was not so lucky. In the final I was allotted the second lane and on this tight-bended track that was, I knew, going to give me a problem. I then behaved stupidly and started moaning and protesting about it. I let it prey on my mind, let the whole business get to me. I suppose it was because I really wanted to achieve the coveted European 'double', but nevertheless, especially after my Rome experiences, I should have known better. Of course, it was clearly wrong for me to be in lane 2 – I had run fastest in both heats and semi-finals – but a cardinal rule is to put all negative thoughts out of your mind and get down to doing the business, which is winning the title.

I finished third, disappointed and disgruntled but cheered slightly by the fact that it was the first time in a major championships that I had completed both sets of races. My British record told me that I was on song for Seoul.

Daley went to California to continue his Olympic preparation in the sunshine. We went to Lanzarote. One morning while we were warming up I noticed a big man in a blazer talking to Ron. He seemed to have a large collection of bags with him. Ron knew him because he was an ex-international shot putter, Dr Martyn Lucking, and he told us that he was there to random dope-test us. 'Hey, guys,' I said, 'look who has come to take the piss out of us!' It received a general laugh and lightened the mood.

I did my test quite happily, joking away with him; I knew that I was clean. Jeff Gutteridge, the pole vaulter, also gave a sample which later proved positive. He was banned for life from competition in the sport by the AAA who, metaphorically speaking, take no prisoners as far as drug abuse is concerned. They do not apply to the IAAF for an athlete's reinstatement.

Martyn's problem was that many of the athletes he was hoping to test were not there. In order to catch the real abusers they have to be a lot quicker, get to the right places, target the right people. There is quite simply no point in random testing women track walkers and marathon runners for steroids during the winter period. It is a waste of time and must bring drug-testing into ridicule.

A cool April evening at West London Stadium. Ron Roddan's group of athletes is busy in the undercover area with their starting practices, among them Wendy Hoyte and Linford. Wendy is an experienced British international athlete of many years' standing. She is about to go to her blocks, the rest watching. 'Make sure,' coach Roddan says to her, 'that you drive off your front foot.'

Linford interrupts. 'Off the front foot?' he says. 'I always drive off the back!'

'I nearly fell over,' Ron said later. 'I thought, "My God! This could be it!" Linford got into his blocks, drove off and he was right, he was only driving off his back foot, which was making his leg crumble a little on the first stride. We had got to the root cause of his starting problem – not quite by accident, but almost. Thank God that for once he had been listening to what I was saying to somebody else! It's a beautiful moment for a coach when something like that happens.'

My first outdoor meeting was at Derby for the UK Championships, where I ran in the 200 metres. I come out early to compete for a specific reason: to show the competition where I am, what standard I have reached. I break training purposely. I run some fast times – I know they will be looking out to see what form I'm in – hopefully faster than my domestic rivals. It gives me a psychological advantage, gives them something to think about while I go back into training again, building up on what I have achieved, ready for the bigger meetings later in the season.

In years of major competition – and three out of four in the Olympic cycle are now such years – everything that you undertake, your training and your competitions, are all geared towards the supreme effort that you intend to make at the appropriate time. The Olympic Games, therefore, have the effect of concentrating the mind wonderfully. I ran a number of meetings in Britain as I had promised, and at the the Peugeot Games at Crystal Palace I beat the Nigerian, Chidi Imo for the first time. This was an important benchmark for me and I was anxious to prove to myself that it was no fluke, and so, completely out of character, I flew to Nice to race him again in the Nikaia Grand Prix meeting. I wanted to prove to myself and, just as importantly, to Chidi – who had run 10 seconds exactly in 1987 – that I was now the better man. I did so by a bigger margin than in London, so I could now write him off my list of challengers for the Olympic Games.

In Nice there was a nostalgic race, the Golden Sprint Memory 200 metres, featuring three grand old men of the track. It was won by Don Quarrie with 21.11, from James Gilkes with 21.39 and Allan Wells with 21.84. All three were over thirty-five years of age. DQ was wonderful. He had run well under 21 seconds in 1988 and was furious not to have made the Jamaican relay team at least.

I respect Don very much, both as an athlete and as a coach. His 200 metre time of 19.96 seconds is still faster than mine, and he set it when I was just eleven years of age. He and Ron are very similar in temperament, not shouting their achievements from the rooftops or constantly searching for the press and television to air their ideas and views. They know about sprinting and let the achievements of their athletes speak for them. Don's knowledge of sprinting is complete and supreme. He was in Seoul coaching Grace Jackson and gave me some help when I came to running in the 200 metres. That is the kind of man he is. They say his ambition is to run under 21 seconds at forty years of age, which, to me, is completely mind-boggling.

The AAA/WAAA Championships in Birmingham promised to be one of the most exciting events of the year, not only because it was the first ever combined Championships but because the British Board's selection policy for the Olympic Games called for the first two in each event (providing they had attained the necessary standard) to be picked, with the selectors being able to exercise their discretion for the third place.

Since it had been announced in January, the selection policy had been strongly criticized by the middle-distance athletes Steve Cram and, more particularly, Sebastian Coe. Coe, one of the greatest of British Olympians, a double winner of the 1500 metres, was, with his father and coach Peter, the supreme architect of Olympic success, timing his preparation to perfection to strike gold on a particular day. The policy advocated by the British Board would negate this approach, requiring Seb to reach his peak earlier in the season in order to be selected. The Board consistently remained adamant that it would stand by its policy, and as the weeks to the meeting became days, so Seb had to search for races to achieve the qualifying standard.

All the top British sprinters were in Birmingham: Regis, McFarlane, Barrington Williams the Pentecostal preacher (normally a long jumper but presently concentrating on the sprints because his religious beliefs prevented him from competing in a Sunday event in Seoul), Elliott Bunney, Clarence Callender. But the man they all had to beat was Linford, in the form of his life, who was again going for a sprint 'double', a feat last achieved by Emmanuel McDonald Bailey, the Trinidadian sprinter who ran for Britain, in 1953.

On all three days the weather was sub-tropical, hot and sunny with barely a trace of wind. The first day of the three-day drama saw the heats and final of the 100 metres.

I was confident about the 100 metres at the Championships, but nervous about John Regis in the 200; he was, after all, the World Championship bronze medallist and he had a good coach in John Isaacs, capable of bringing him to form at the right time. It is always disappointing to me that they run the shorter sprint on the Friday, usually in the cool of the evening thus precluding fast times and, incidentally, upping the chances of injury. They say it is traditional, but surely the popularity and standard of the event should be more important considerations. On the Friday the crowd was small. In the final I won from John Regis with Barrington Williams snatching third place. The time was my fastest of the year: 10.15 seconds. In the 200 metres on the Sunday, I felt really very smooth indeed and won in 20.46 seconds into a headwind. Although I didn't realize it, the race behind me more closely resembled a battlefield, with John Regis and Donovan Reid spreadeagled across the track. In the end John was stretchered off, but suffering only from cramp. Donovan's injury was more serious. I was absolutely delighted to have achieved the first sprint 'double' in thirty-five years.

I agreed in principle with the selection policy, although I believe it should have had some flexibility for exceptional circumstances built into it. Such a policy gave everybody a fair chance of going to the Olympic Games, which is still the ambition of every athlete. It was announced early in the year so that for many months everyone knew what they had to do to gain selection: go to Birmingham for the Championships and be placed in the first two. With this system somebody always comes through who would not otherwise have been selected. An example of that was young Michael Rosswess, who came third in the 200 metres. I am sure he would not have been picked if there had been pre-selection, yet he was to make the Olympic final.

I do not believe in pre-selection, but think that everybody should prove themselves. My philosophy is that you cannot call yourself the best until you have run against and beaten everybody else. When I felt that the old system had weighed against me I complained bitterly, because I believed that I deserved a chance and was not getting it because athletes were being pre-selected. I just wish that there had been Trials in my formative years as a world-class athlete. In addition, I think that Trials actually help to prevent injury. It stops athletes going to lesser events and it concentrates their minds and makes them take that extra care with their fitness because the stakes are so high.

Of course, the new system wasn't perfect. I was totally dis-

Above: A supreme
moment! Winning the
1986 European 100 metres
title in 10.15 seconds ahead
of Bringmann of East
Germany and Marie-Rose
of France

Right: A happier moment
in Rome with my coach,
Ron Roddan

Above left: Winning for Great Britain in the 1987 European Cup in Prague

Above right: Celebrating a win at the 1987 Miller Lite meeting at Crystal Palace

Left: Qualifying with Ben Johnson in the semi-final of the 1987 World Championships in Rome. Ben set a world record in the final. I came fourth

Opposite page

Above: My first Olympic final – at the start in Seoul

Below left: Celebrating an Olympic relay silver with Mike McFarlane, John Regis and Elliott Bunney

Below right: Savouring the moment! Talking to Kevin Cosgrove for the BBC after the 100 metres final

Finish of the most sensational Olympic 100 metres ever. Ben Johnson wins but is later disqualified for failing a drugs test. I'm on my way to an eventual silver and am the first European under ten seconds

gusted by what happened in the women's javelin. Here was an event in which Tessa Sanderson and Fatima Whitbread were metres ahead of the opposition. But both were injured, and with no announcement from the BAAB it seemed likely that one could be left out of the team for Seoul if they did not compete. Sharon Gibson would probably win the Trial, but if Julie Abel threw the qualifying distance then she would be in the team and either Tessa or Fatima would be excluded. Although she had beaten Fatima all season, Tessa was aware that it was very likely the selectors would pick Fatima for the vacant third spot, if for no other reason than that she was the world champion.

Tessa arrived in Birmingham with a bad foot injury and in a distressed state. She and Joan Watt went out to the warm-up area, with the media in attendance, to try out her foot. Joan Allison, the women's assistant manager, was very supportive, and I went up to Tessa as she was hobbling around on the synthetic grass and told her not to throw. 'Why should you bail out the Board?' I asked her. 'Let them save their own face.' In the end that point of view prevailed, and she did not throw. There was more interest in the javelin that afternoon than in almost any other event. If Julie Abel had thrown the qualifying distance (she came within 150 centimetres of doing so) then the BAAB would have been in grave danger of being a world laughing stock.

Seb Coe not qualifying for the final of the 1500 metres caused another furore. I didn't really understand what the problem was. A good, fit Seb would have won the Trial easily. But he was not in that condition.

At a press conference before we went to Seoul I remember specifically *not* being asked about the non-selection of Seb Coe. Next day in the tabloids the headlines screamed: 'Linford Christie Says That Seb Coe And Steve Cram Should Stop Moaning.' Luckily both Steve and Seb had been through all this before and they tend to ignore anything that is written about them.

The words that the press report us as saying include some that I would never use. They frequently credit black people with using the word 'man'. I never say it. Scottish people use it more than the black community in England does, yet the tabloids insist on using 'man' every time they quote (or more likely misquote) a black person. I was also once quoted on the subject of the leotards that many of our women athletes wear nowadays. They credited me with saying, 'Girls in leotards make me go hot and cold.' I didn't even understand it. What does it mean, I asked everybody. It is an expression that I have never used.

We all suffer from the press. The more successful you are, the more it becomes one of life's hazards. But I thought that the *Daily Mirror's* treatment of Peter Elliott in the weeks leading up to the Olympics was the lowest form of gutter journalism. I'm told that years ago the *Mirror* had one of Fleet Street's great sports reporters, Peter Wilson. I am sure that the treatment of Peter Elliott would have made him positively spin in his grave. The 'Seb Must Go' campaign and the depicting of Peter as a cart-horse was surely the product of warped minds, and totally misdirected. Peter was the world silver medallist from Rome, and if anyone deserved to be in Seoul it was he. I understand that the sports editor of the *Mirror* said that it was all supposed to be harmless fun, which says a lot more about him than about Peter Elliott. Luckily Peter is a tough, down-to-earth Yorkshireman, worthy of his nickname the 'Tough of the Track'. Although the *Mirror* articles hurt, he was able to rise above it and perform marvellously in Seoul.

No other press in the world treats its athletes and sports stars in the way that the British press does. And even before we left for Seoul, the hacks were sharpening their pencils and licking their lips in anticipation of what they could write, and if necessary invent, about British Olympic hopefuls. In recent years a new breed of hack had been born – the sports news journalist, whose very last concern was British success; dishing the dirt was the name of the game.

I ran at the Zurich meeting, which every athlete seems to take so seriously. I clocked 10.07 seconds and finished fifth! It was a complete and total shock to my system. What kind of race is this, I asked my astounded self. Carl won it and was ecstatic; Calvin was second, and he was very happy too; Ben was third and totally depressed. Chidi, in fourth place, was happy to have beaten me again. And I, Linford Christie, was dumbstruck. I mean, 10.07 was not a time to be sneezed at. I was the only person in Britain to have run faster, and yet I had finished fifth. As you can see, it got to me – still does. Later, however, in a cooler frame of mind, I was pleased with my performance. It indicated that I was improving all the time. Come Seoul I would be ready.

Ben had had a depressing year altogether, mainly through

injury. Up until this race he had held the psychological advantage over Carl, winning the last six races. Carl hadn't beaten him since the Cologne Grand Prix of 1985. The lure of reportedly very big money indeed had brought Ben to the Weltklasse, but now it was Carl who was in the driving seat. Ben then decided to return to Canada to recover and try to get his act together in the remaining six weeks before Seoul.

The amount of money supposedly offered to Ben and Carl to race at Zurich – half a million dollars – caused a lot of anger among the athletes. The American contingent called a meeting at the Nova Park Hotel to discuss the situation. A couple of us went along, mainly to hear everybody's point of view and not to enter into any dispute. I thought that it was a good idea all the athletes coming together for such a discussion; a policy of divide and rule by the promoters had been in operation for too long.

The press members were alerted. The promoter, Andreas Bruger, came in and tried to explain the situation. He told the meeting that he had gone out of his way to invite more American athletes than any other promoter, which instantly annoyed all the non-Americans there. The man heading the meeting was the sprinter Harvey Glance. I stood by Willie Banks, the triple jumper, and made no contribution; neither did he. We kept in the background, but *The Times* reporter in Zurich, Pat Butcher, wrote that I was an instigator of the meeting, which was completely untrue.

Strong denials were later issued that Carl and Ben had shared the half-million, but it was slightly reminiscent of the Zola Budd saga in 1985 when she had received £90,000 for running against Mary Decker. There had been initial denials then that she had received such a sum of money, but it had later transpired that it had come from American television. I suspect that the same situation obtained in Zurich. Nevertheless, it seemed incredible to me that they should have been receiving sums forty or fifty times greater than those enjoyed by Calvin, Chidi, Dennis Mitchell and me.

Andy Norman looks after us to an extent. It may be that we could get better deals, but it is also true that we could get a lot worse. He makes sure that over a season our livelihood is taken care of. Certainly, he produced all the opposition for me in 1988. I could not have avoided anyone even if I had wanted to. I raced Dennis Mitchell and Chidi Imo; abroad I faced Calvin Smith,

Ben and Carl. Sometimes I won and sometimes I lost, but it was an excellent learning process and it enabled me to gain in confidence all the time. The important factor in it all was that by the time I arrived in Seoul I would have run against all the main opposition, so none of them would hold any fears for me.

The television commentators were saying that I was racing too much, and once one of the media makes a comment like that it becomes an accepted truth. Ron, for once, became very angry. He made a statement: 'I would like to reassure everyone, including TV viewers, that he is not over-racing, for the simple fact is that all races so far have been part of his training programme. He has also run less races than in previous years and I would have thought that experienced athletes such as Ovett and Hutchings [who were the commentators] would have realized what the situation was like before making comments on it; or they could have asked Linford or myself.'

After the Trials a group of us, including Colin Jackson, his coach Malcolm Arnold, Malcolm's wife, Madeline, Sally-Ann Short, Lesley-Anne Skeet and myself travelled to Nice for a week's training. Malcolm is the only coach apart from Ron with whom I would go abroad training. Colin and he are genuine people. I believe that Malcolm is a brilliant coach, very analytical and honest. Training with them is like being with a family; I join them and just fit in. They are very knowledgeable and we analyse each other thoroughly; we are unstinting in our criticism, but we all accept it.

It was a good week's training in the balmy Mediterranean sunshine. The days were now slipping away before our departure, first to the holding camp in Japan and then on to Seoul. We had had our inoculations and collected our uniforms (with which I was totally unimpressed). Our final domestic meeting was at Crystal Palace, the McVitie's Challenge. Thomas Jefferson just beat me on a photo-finish in the 100 metres, but we both clocked the same time. It was not an important race, just a case of flying the flag before we flew to Seoul. It was Allan Wells' last appearance; he came sixth, but that was not significant either. What was important was that the sport and his public gave him a good send-off, and that they certainly did, cheering him on a farewell lap of honour. Allan had made a tremendous contribution to British sprinting, made especially so by the fact that at the time, the sport was in the doldrums. Olympic champion, Commonwealth champion and World Cup winner – these are wonderful trophies and memories to take with you into retirement.

Allan had tipped Calvin Smith to take the gold medal in the 100 metres. Bookmakers William Hill quoted me at 25 to 1 for gold. Everyone was getting excited about the Olympics. The gear was packed, the farewells said. We were to be away for just over a month. My next competitions would be in the vast Olympic Stadium in Seoul in the most important races of my life.

13
Japanese Hold-up

We flew via Anchorage to Tokyo. It was a long flight, full of other Olympians – many from other sports including quite a few swimmers. The journey – about twelve hours in total – was marred by journalists, some of whom I had never seen before, who smoked and drank heavily as they sat among the athletes. One in particular made himself extremely obnoxious, literally staggering around the plane looking for Tom McKean. Tom had had a rough time with the *Sun* newspaper prior to his coming out when they had printed a story concerning an alleged visit to a night club in Scotland, a confessional-type piece of the 'I spent a night with Tom McKean' variety. He tried to interview one of the swimmers believing that he was Tom, and he was well into it before he realized he was being taken for a ride. He came up to me, pushed his face close to mine, his breath reeking of alcohol, and asked, 'Are you on drugs?'

'I could kill a man for saying a lot less than that,' I replied, and he reeled away.

The athletics correspondent of the same newspaper, came up shortly afterwards full of apologies, and he and one or two of the others eventually managed to steer him away.

We landed at Tokyo airport and were whisked away about sixty miles or so east to the Nihon Aerobics Centre, near Chiba, a magnificent structure and quite the best training centre I have ever seen. The facilities were out of this world: a complete 400 metre synthetic track with weight-training facilities in the centre. The Aerobics Centre itself was three floors high, with dining hall and reception on the ground floor, lecture rooms, medical rooms, saunas and jacuzzis on the first floor, and a sports hall and swimming pool with strength-training equipment on the top floor. The whole facility cost upwards of half a billion pounds.

Frank Dick had chosen this centre for our holding camp, a period of time for us to recuperate and then prepare for the Games away from the hurly-burly and stresses of the Olympic Village. It was a magnificent choice, although Frank had to take a lot of criticism from people who wanted to know why we had chosen to stay in Japan and not in Korea. All credit to him for that.

There was, however, one major snag. When we arrived – we were the second group in from Britain – we discovered, to our shock and anger, the press already fully installed. After our experiences on the flight out it was the last thing we wanted. Everyone was there, all the athletics correspondents, newspaper photographers, BBC and ITV television representatives, and independent radio reporters. In addition there were about five hundred Japanese media people (or there appeared to be), mostly photographers and television crews, filming and photographing all day long. It was absolutely incredible. No one had informed the athletes, let alone consulted us as to whether we approved or minded. It was simply a *fait accompli* on our arrival. The main problem of having the press with us at the camp and on the plane was that we could never relax. It had been a long flight, and while athletes and swimmers get on well together we had been worried about being observed all the time, worried that the slightest innocent action could have been misconstrued. The same would now apply at the Aerobics Centre.

After a couple of days of acclimatization we settled down to training, but then some very unpleasant rumours began to emanate from the athletics correspondents. They said that they had been joined by another reporter who was in fact from the *News of the World*. Worse still, he was wandering around asking a lot of questions about Tessa Sanderson and me. His name was John Chapman.

We couldn't believe it, and by the time we received the tip-off he had completed his story and checked out of the Centre. Often you are unaware of events happening to or around you until later, and then the penny drops. Suddenly Tessa and I remembered that at Heathrow there had been photographers asking, 'Can we take pictures of you and Tessa together?' We had agreed. We are two senior members of the team after all, and we are also friends. They had taken photographs all over the place, inside and outside Terminal 4, and had shouted, 'Put your arm around her, Linford!' in their usual way. We also remembered that at the Birmingham Championships, when Tessa was in a really bad way about the javelin event, I had gone over with the women team managers Pam Piercy and Joan Allison to give her advice and comfort. Again the photographers had been milling around, and we supposed that it was from all that that the paper had decided upon its story.

While he was at Nihon, Chapman saw Tom McKean in the showers, so he stripped off, joined him and tried to interview him about the piece in the *Sun*. He was clearly on an assignment to write a juicy, gossipy story from Japan.

A photographer at Nihon was instructed to take some pictures of Tessa and me together. Colin was with us in the middle of the track, and we were relaxing and enjoying ourselves, fooling about. He took his pictures, and then when they printed them they cut Colin out. The photograph was entitled 'Floored by Passion'! It was really so ridiculous that although we were angry we had to chuckle as well.

The athletics media were very put out about this intrusion, and quite rightly because it only heightened the team's annoyance at the press being present and made us more uncooperative in the matter of interviews.

We waited to see what story would be printed in the *News of the World*. 'My God,' we said to each other, 'what is he going to write?' Finally a copy of his piece was faxed through from London. It was all passion-in-the-bushes journalism. He wrote that we had disappeared for six hours into the woods after training, which anybody who was at Nihon would know was impossible, security being so tight. He wrote that we were having a marvellously sexy affair. It was all so outlandish that we realized, with relief, that nobody would take it seriously – and who would care, anyway?

But what if either of us had been married? Tom McKean had fortunately found his girlfriend supportive when the story about him appeared in the *Sun*, but we would have had a job convincing wives or husbands twelve thousand miles away that the *News of the World* story was a fabrication.

The media became angry because nobody wanted to talk to them and they were obviously under pressure from their editors in London. Tessa and I finally agreed to give a press conference. We did this after talking at length to Pam Piercy and Joan Allison. They were both wonderful to Tessa and me, highly supportive, but then they are excellent team managers. Both are ex-international 800 metre runners and still remember what it was like when they were competing. If you had problems, they were the ones you would turn to, almost like mother figures. Unfortunately nobody told us that Pam was retiring after the Olympics, so we never had the opportunity to express our thanks to her in a tangible form.

Before we answered questions from the press we had a frank exchange of views and told them exactly what we thought. 'Encouragement strengthens labour,' I told them, quoting a saying of my father's, 'but where is the encouragement from you guys? Constant criticism demoralizes athletes and encourages the opposition.' They all nodded, but all they wanted to do was get on with the questions.

I avoid tabloid journalists as much as I can. That type of newspaper sickens me, pandering to people's worst instincts. As athletics has gained a higher profile, so its participants have had to suffer from the attentions of the worst kind of reporters. The British press now have the lowest reputation in the world, on a par with our football supporters. I just don't understand why the public put up with it, in some cases encourage it. I've been in Britain for twenty-one years, and I still cannot fathom it.

Of course, I must not tar them all with the same brush. John Rodda of the *Guardian* has never written a bad word about any athlete. His criticism is constructive; he knows his athletics. If John criticizes you then you know you have probably done something wrong. Neil Wilson of the *Independent* and Cliff Temple of the *Sunday Times* are two others, along with Kenny Mays of the *Daily Telegraph* and Randall Northam of *Athletics Today*, and a few others who all seem to take a constructive approach to what is happening. Others, though, even some of the 'serious' journalists, are always looking for controversy, and never seem to write anything but criticism.

I do not often talk to the press, for one simple reason: for the following twenty-four hours I worry intensely about what is going to appear. Will I be misquoted or misconstrued? Worse still, will I have a quote attributed to me that I haven't said at all? I can really do without that kind of hassle. Finally, I wonder about the mentality of some of the tabloid reporters. Are they married men? Do they have children? Do they allow their children to see and read what appears in their papers or what they have written? Some of their children must, like all kids, have their own sporting heroes. Do these journalists delight in toppling their kids' idols from pedestals, in making their children as cynical as they are, just in the name of selling a few more copies?

The salient fact that the press failed to grasp at Nihon was that the athletes did not differentiate between the correspondents on the front page and those on the back. Nor did they want to. Tom McKean, Tessa Sanderson and Linford had been the subjects of sleaze journalism, and it was now evident that certain sections of the media were considering the Olympics and all those associated with them to be fair game for that type of reporting and fictionalizing. Back in London, editors and some sports editors were instituting policies that flew in the face of their reporters' needs in Japan. There was a conflict of interests that the reporters at Nihon seemed unwilling or unable to transmit back to their papers.

While the British athletics team trained quietly at Nihon, the media monsters of Maxwell's and Murdoch's papers were already unleashed and scurrying around Seoul eager to write stories that were a total antithesis of what the spirit of human endeavour in sport is all about.

We could not have had better preparation for the Games than we got at Nihon. We could train when we liked during the day, and the team could relax and get to know each other better. We all made new friends, shared problems, gave advice. Ron was with me – only just, however, he nearly didn't make it through an administrative slip – and we worked together with Colin Jackson and Malcolm Arnold. A gang of us gradually congregated together – Sally Gunnell, Dalton Grant, Joanne Mulliner, Kim Hagger, Myrtle Augee, Tessa, John Herbert – and we had a lot of fun and laughs, which helped us get through the pre-Olympic tension that seemed to be affecting one or two of the others. This all carried on into Seoul and Sally and Dalton later said that it reminded them of their days with the Junior International team, carefree times which they thought had disappeared for ever.

Our living accommodation was in chalets scattered among pine trees, away from the Centre to which mini-buses shuttled us throughout the day. I shared with Colin because we are very similar in temperament and understand each other very well. The last people I would ever want to share with would be fellow sprinters. I don't socialize with any of them. I believe that it would be a fatal flaw in my armoury; I couldn't psych myself up to beat people I was very friendly with.

The food at Nihon was excellent; served buffet style, it would have been a credit to any Park Lane hotel. At every meal there was a selection of first-class fish and meat dishes, together with salads and mountains of fruit. We were able to relax a little more at meal times because the media had a separate section of the dining area.

It rained a good deal of the time but the weather was also very humid, and if there is one thing that sprinters like, apart from hot and sunny days, it is heavy humidity. If you jogged only a little you would break into a sweat, and then you knew that your muscles were really warm and loose and that you could run flat-out without any fear of injury. I carried out starting practice with Colin and Barrington Williams and was highly encouraged by my efforts.

Behind an escort of police motor cyclists with wailing sirens, the United States team arrived at Nihon by coach from the airport. Japanese photographers and television crews milled about for hours beforehand in a permanent state of anxiety, for they were awaiting Flo-Jo, Florence Griffith-Joyner, the woman who had set a phenomenal new world-record of 10.49 seconds for the 100 metres at the US Olympic Trials. It was a time that had been greeted with scepticism by large sections of the athletics world. Linford said that he remembered when he was running 10.5 and could not conceive of her running faster and beating him. In the previous year only thirteen British men had sprinted a faster time than she had.

But Flo-Jo was more than the fastest woman on earth. She was glamour personified, with her colourful make-up and her running costumes which had electrified the public and set new fashions for women athletes. At Nihon she and her husband Al were followed around almost continuously by reverential cameras recording her every move and gesture. Her press conference was conducted amid a persistent cacophony of clicking camera shutters. In charge was the highly inscrutable, totally humourless public relations man of the Centre, Ichiro Kawato. Flo-Jo sat there in the spotlights, as immobile as a Madame Tussaud waxwork, stirring only to answer the mostly inane questions: 'Flo-Jo, please tell us how you keep so pretty?' She gave an almost equally inane answer about personal appearance, and then lapsed back into her dummy-like state, studying her fabulously long, fabulously red fingernails.

Carl Lewis's conference was an altogether different affair. He had been smuggled into the camp quietly, away from the rest of the team. He sat facing the media members with his diminutive manager Joe Douglas. 'Stand up, Joe! Stand up!' the British pressmen shouted to Douglas, who was standing. 'Mr Carl Lewis, please stand up,' said the Nihon PR man expressionlessly. Carl stood amid a buzz of shutters. 'What is this,' he asked, 'The Dating Game?' He answered all questions deftly. Yes, he was in the best shape of his life; yes, he was confident after beating Ben Johnson at Zurich. All he could really say was that he would do his very best.

I watched the Americans arrive. Suddenly a glaring light shone, a camera began to roll, a microphone appeared in front of me. 'Carl Lewis is here,' snapped a man from ITN. 'Have you anything to say to him?' It was ridiculous and discourteous asking such a question without any warning.

Carl and I had had an exchange in Sestriere in Italy. There had been the usual back-biting beforehand in the pre-race tension and we had said a few hard words to each other. The press had picked it up and when we met again in Zurich, we shook hands and both apologized. I had sought out Joe Douglas in the hotel and explained the situation to him. It was all a quite gentlemanly business. But the press, as ever, wrote that Carl had offered me the olive branch and that I had snapped it!

Having the Americans at Nihon added zest to our final preparations. At any time on the track you might come across Ed Moses, majestic as ever, Calvin Smith or Carl, Butch Reynolds, the new world-record holder for 400 metres, Flo-Jo or, from our side, Steve Cram, Liz McColgan, Daley or Colin. Seeing all those people there, training hard and earnestly, you knew that the Olympic Games were now not very far away. I watched Calvin at starting practice and did not think that he was looking exceptionally dynamic, and that helped my confidence. The Americans were watching us as well, so that made us train just that little bit harder. My starts were improving all the time; I was frequently up with Colin and Barrington now over the first fifteen metres.

One incident has stayed with me. On the track was an American who had run much faster than I had done for 200 metres. But his build was totally different from mine, short and stocky. He seemed an odd shape. I looked at him and I thought, bloody hell, there is something wrong here, here am I in the best shape of my life, tall, narrow, strong, and here is this funny-shaped guy that can run so much faster than I can. I thought, I can't be doing the right thing, I'm going wrong somewhere; there is no way that this guy should be running faster than I am! I brooded on that for a long time!

Television took some film of us training for transmission on sports programmes back home. Kevin Cosgrove was there for the BBC and Jim Rosenthal for ITV, and both were very considerate, fully understanding our needs and knowing when to approach and when not to.

Tessa suffered a bad injury to her heel, opening up an old scar, while she was training on a field away from the Centre. Two of our throwers carried her back, her heel dripping blood, and rushed into the lobby past astonished pressmen and up to the second floor to receive medical treatment. The aftermath of the incident created further tension with the media who were demanding to know the extent of the injury, while the management, aided by a few of us, were trying to be as protective as possible of Tessa. Although she travelled on to Seoul, the injury really finally ruined her chances of successfully defending her title in the javelin. It had been a sad year for her.

Towards the end of our stay at Nihon, monotony set in. I was beginning to feel claustrophobic. The Japanese Red Army had threatened both the Americans and us and the authorities were not taking any chances. There was barbed wire around the perimeter of the grounds, and armed guards in evidence. There was nowhere for us to travel to, for the Nihon Centre is well out into the countryside. Some athletes did get away for competitions at a stadium in Chiba, but I did not enter. I was beginning to understand how prisoners of war must feel. A Korean folk night was laid on for us and there were numerous books and videos, but the need to get out into the world again and mix with people was growing stronger every day.

Problems were arising about the relay teams, the 4 × 400 metres, as well as the sprint, but I had learnt my lesson and kept well away from all the discussion and argument. I had my priority set this time – the 100 metres. Frank called relay practices and I attended one or two. There were still the old uncertainties about the running order. Frank still had me running second, and there was a disgruntled air about the squad. The reserves we had with us were very inexperienced and it was clear that they would not be making the final four. Again I felt that Frank should have named the team, so that people could have relaxed and got on with their preparation properly.

The uncertainty seemed to centre around Mike McFarlane. Strong rumours abounded, the more persistent of which put it about that Frank wanted to leave Mac out of the team. He hadn't had a brilliant season to say the least, and this was obviously weighing with Frank. The running order being touted about was Bunney, Christie, Regis and then Mac or Clarence Callender. Clarence had had a lot of experience on the final leg, so Mac, who can be a moody person anyway, was in the doldrums. I felt that it would be crazy to leave Mac out of the team. He was the most experienced relay runner that we had and one of the best bend runners in the world. Regardless of how indifferent his individual form is, put a relay baton in his hand and he is a world beater – very similar in a way to Phil Brown in the longer relay. I also had strong thoughts on my running the second leg, but I kept all of those to myself.

A trip was arranged for us to go to Disneyland – Japanese style – and it was a relief for everybody to get away from the Aerobics Centre. ITV made a contribution towards the trip but, of course, that meant having the cameras with us. However, everyone was so relieved just to escape that it didn't really matter.

Finally came the day of the Opening Ceremony in Seoul. We watched it on television. I think a lot of athletes would have liked to have been in Korea, especially those whose first Olympics this was. A fair number of the team believed quite strongly that we should have had the choice, because for some these would be their only Games. My own feelings were tempered by the fact that I thought that the British Olympic uniform was tatty.

The team did not look as good as it should have done as it marched in the opening parade. The Russians looked excellent in double-breasted suits: the Bulgarians, too, looked very smart. Looking good means feeling good, and when the British teams begin to look inferior to the rest of the world, then something is very wrong. I felt the same in Stuttgart, where I believed that our tracksuits looked cheap and nasty. One of the conditions of companies being awarded a contract to supply British teams with gear should be that they provide them with the best possible. I hope that this happens in future, so that our teams can make people feel proud to see them.

Once the Games were under way everyone wanted to be in Seoul, to be where the action was, even though the track and field events would not start until the eighth day. My preparation had gone perfectly at Nihon, so I would have no excuses. I had a lot of people to thank for bringing me to the greatest physical and mental condition of my life: Ron, of course, Malcolm, Colin and Daley. The staff at the Aerobics Centre, with their boss Toshi and manager Tadashi, gathered to see us go. Every one of them looked totally fatigued, ready for a year's sleep. They had coped magnificently with us and all our diverse needs. Nothing was ever too much trouble for them.

Now the pace was quickening. We climbed into the coach and were driven up the motorway to Tokyo, into the hustle and bustle of one of the busiest airports in the world. The flight to Seoul was just two hours.

14
Looking Good

After the teams had been welcomed by smiling, happy Koreans at Seoul's Kimpo airport, they were driven on a motorway that ran alongside the Han River. The first building they would see of the big, sprawling city of ten million people was the huge, gold-tinted skyscraper of the Daehan Insurance Company on Yoido Island, once the tallest building in Asia. Then the city itself would come into view, built on a number of hills on the north side of the Han. All Seoul's history, since it was founded in 1392 right up until the beginning of the 1980s, had its origins on this northern side of the river. The southern side, once a wasteland, had been developed only in recent years, although more rapidly since the Korean capital had been awarded the Olympic Games in 1982.

Then, as the city passed by on the left, so in front the Olympic Stadium would appear, a magnificent piece of architecture made more dramatic after nightfall by its muted floodlighting. Finally the coaches would arrive at the Olympic Village, a vast, concrete complex heavily guarded by the South Korean army and manned by a volunteer force of young people in brightly coloured blazers of varying hues. Security was tight – there was a paranoid fear of North Korean terrorists – but always polite, for the Korean people maintained throughout the Games, despite many provocations, their Confucian and Buddhist spirit of gentility and courtesy.

On a hot Saturday morning in mid September, coaches carrying the competitors and officials from 161 countries bore down on the Olympic Stadium and parked in a vast, dusty car park by the Han. A few hours later in a packed stadium, with thousands of competitors, many in national dress, assembled on the grass infield of the red synthetic track, President Roh Tae Woo declared open the Games of the XXIVth Olympiad of the Modern Era.

A few days later the first contingent of Great Britain's athletics team, now to be integrated into the British Olympic Team under Team Commandant Charles Palmer and Chef de Mission Dick Palmer, moved into the Village.

Living in the Village was like how I imagined it must be living in one of the council estates that were built in Britain in the sixties, high-rise blocks of concrete flats with no character. However, inside they were comfortable enough. We had to change all the rooming arrangements – the administrators have not yet realized that sprinters do not like sharing with each other. In our particular section on the ninth and top floors were John Herbert, Dalton Grant, Matt Mileham, David Ottley, with Colin and me, as ever, sharing a room.

The weather was very hot in the daytime, cool in the evening, and the security was immense with double and triple checks as you entered the campus from outside. We ate in a large, glass-sided restaurant on two floors which was open for twenty-four hours a day, but mostly we had to queue which was a bore. The food was acceptable, but we really had been spoilt at the Nihon Centre. The saving grace was the vast quantity of fruit.

I had flown into the Olympics with a big worry: a strained abductor muscle. Ron had had to return to Britain from Japan, but I had Malcolm to rely on and we used a training track well away from the Village, away from the media. It was just as well, for at my first session I couldn't run more than thirty metres before breaking down. This is it, I thought, my first Olympics and I'm going to be completely sidelined by injury. Andy Norman urged, 'You've come all this way; get out there and bloody run!' Frank Dick advised me to 'run through it'. From the moment I arrived in Seoul Frank was marvellous, extremely helpful. It was as if nothing had ever happened between us.

The night before the heats of the 100 metres I hardly slept at all with the worry of my injury. I know my body, and I know that if I don't have aches and pains before a major race then I'm not going to run well; that if I feel perfect I'm going to have a problem. But this was different; this was a specific injury to a specific muscle.

I must have slept a little, because I remember waking up! It was very, very early but dawn had broken. I felt extremely nervous, and when I went to the restaurant I couldn't eat. I felt so tired and couldn't stop yawning. I thought, my God, this is no good. Malcolm kept urging me to eat, but all I could manage was four cups of coffee. 'Hey,' said Malcolm, 'you'll get banned for caffeine if you go on like that.' We laughed. He really was a great morale-booster.

I arrived at the stadium early and had a massage from Joan Watt. We had a good chat while she worked away, and that helped me relax some more. She is a real mother figure to the athletes, always ending up a session by reminding us to check our shoelaces! I met Joe Douglas in the warm-up area and we walked a little. I waved at Carl. Going through the motions of my one-and-a-half-hour warm-up routine, I was worrying all the time about the niggle in my abductor. Will it stand up, or will I crash out of the Games in the first round? I eased down on my practice starts.

On my way through the checking procedures with Les Jones, the assistant team manager, I went to the lavatory two or three times, which is fairly normal. I had the young East German Matthes in my heat and I knew he was a fast starter, so I concentrated hard, thinking about my own start and pick-up. I followed him out, went into the lead and won. It was so easy that I felt wonderful: my injury had disappeared.

Linford had been in the fifth heat of ten and won in 10.19 seconds, the fastest so far. The stadium was half empty for this first morning of the athletics events, and as the thirteen heats (to reduce a field of ninety-four to forty-eight) evolved it was obvious that there were to be no surprises. Ben Johnson, Calvin Smith, Dennis Mitchell, Ray Stewart and Desai Williams all qualified easing down. In the final heat Carl Lewis cruised in at 10.14 seconds, the fastest time of the round. Of the other British competitors John Regis, caught out by an athlete in the next lane stumbling and falling, failed to qualify. Barrington Williams had gone through, third in his heat. During the morning's athletics Jackie Joyner-Kersee, sister-in-law of Flo-Jo, had run an amazing 12.69 seconds in the 100 metres hurdles of the heptathlon, faster than any British hurdler had ever run. Linford, meanwhile, had a three-hour wait until he was to sprint again.

I went back out to the warm-up track and had a further massage, as I always do. Frank Dick brought across the draw for the second-round heats and I discovered that I was running against Ben. I had no worries – they had dissolved in 10.19 seconds. Dennis Mitchell was also in my heat, but there was nobody else of note. I idled the time away for a while, speaking to that great American sprinter Evelyn Ashford, who was not racing until the next day.

We were in the first heat. Ben blazed away to his usual start, but with ten metres to go it appeared to me that he had nothing more to give. I ran in to win, and Dennis Mitchell also went past him. It meant that Ben was in the galling position of having to wait to see if he would be one of the four fastest losers. My time was 10.11 seconds.

It was the first time that I had ever been close to Ben, let alone beaten him, which was an enormous psychological boost for me; and I had clocked the second-fastest time of the round. I went through my usual post-race routine and then headed for the Village, absolutely exhausted. It may be only a hundred metres and ten seconds, but it takes an enormous amount out of you, both physically and emotionally. By this time, I was also very hungry – I had completed two rounds of the Olympic Games on four cups of coffee!

Our crowd all had dinner together and everyone was full of enthusiasm and encouragement. Then I went to bed, very tired. It had been a wonderful day for me and I felt on top of the world.

Ben Johnson had qualified for the semi-final by being the fastest loser with 10.17 seconds. The pundits were all agreed, however, that his chances of winning the gold medal the next day looked remote, that he had spoilt his chances with that injudicious race against Lewis in Zurich. In the Weltklasse he had clearly not recovered from his early-season injuries, and by running there he had increased the time needed to get back to full fitness. Lewis had the psychological advantage, and in his second-round heat he had rammed that home by running the fastest overall time of the event so far, 9.99 seconds. That in essence, was the theory. Lewis looked set to retain his Olympic crown.

Linford had surprised everybody with two wins and the second-fastest time of the day. He had beaten both Johnson and Mitchell, two medal contenders, and it seemed that he was a certainty to reach the final. Ron Roddan, watching bleary-eyed in London, agreed absolutely with that prognosis. This was a totally different man from the one who had competed in Rome twelve months earlier.

The 100 metres final was as dramatic and exciting as everyone had thought it would be. Ben Johnson had fooled everybody again – including Carl Lewis who for the second year in succession had run the fastest time of his life and set a new American record of 9.92 seconds, but still finished second. Lewis said, 'I ran a pretty good race – although not excellent. I was three lanes away from Ben so I did not see him until sixty or seventy metres. I ran the best race I possibly could.' For the first time in history, four men had bettered ten seconds in one race; Calvin Smith, in fourth place, was timed at 9.99 seconds.

Afterwards there were chaotic scenes, both in doping control and in the press interview room which proved totally inadequate for the occasion. Each of the medallists went separately for their interviews, which had to be conducted in three languages. The Korean organizers had never imagined the enormous global interest the race would create.

Much later, in the corridors that stretched underneath the vast concrete stands, Carl and Joe Douglas were wandering in a daze, desperately looking for a quiet way out to the sacrosanct warm-up track where they would be safe from the frantic media.

The former Olympic champion just stared ahead, his dreams of immortality gone. Still, in modern Olympic history, no man had successfully defended a 100 metres title.

I ate quite a lot that night, and I was sore. It is the shock of everything – getting up so early in the morning, two major races in one day in front of packed crowds and millions watching round the world, the interviews with the press and television, and all virtually on an empty stomach, because there was nothing much to eat at the stadium. You keep going on an emotional high, but when you stop and relax – poof! You go out like a light. You are in the very best shape of your life, but then your body says, hey! I need a rest. It will take so much, but finally it makes its protest.

Everyone was showering me with congratulations, both at the stadium and in the Village. People from other countries and other sports were coming up and shaking my hand. When I went to my room I found a big white polar bear on my bed, left for me by Myrtle Augee and the group. It was a wonderful evening. But there weren't too many celebrations, because I knew that I still had the 200 metres to come.

A sprinter trains all year round, in all weathers, for just two or three main races a year. I had truly suffered, with the distance work and the runs at 300 metres and 400 metres at West London Stadium, in Lanzarote and in Nice, under the unrelenting eyes of Ron Roddan and Daley Thompson. At those times I had said to myself, 'If I've got to hurt like this, then the opposition is going to pay for it!' I had gone through all that, hours and hours of it, for the privilege of running just under ten seconds in Seoul.

I had exactly forty-five hours between my 100 metres final and the opening heats of the 200 – much less if you take away the time spent on all the fuss over the first event and preparations for the second. I was still sore and tired when I awoke on the Sunday morning. When you are racing and training all the time you often become run down and your immune system is affected. I'd taken vitamin supplements ever since they had been recommended by Anna-Lisa Hammer, and I had also been taking ginseng. Ginseng is a natural root and among its medicinal effects is replacing lost energy, lowering stress and generally perking you up. It is also supposed to increase sexual awareness – but I have to report that in that regard it hasn't done much for me. The Orientals have been taking ginseng for centuries.

The first ginseng that I took was Red Koog, in a tablet form. Then one day I went into a health shop and the assistant recommended that I take the ginseng in liquid form rather than tablets. I tried it and it tasted fine, as it included honey. The tablets had tasted really revolting, and although my grandmother used to tell me that a medicine never did you any good unless it tasted nasty, I was very happy to switch. Anyway, liquids are absorbed into the system a lot more easily than tablets. The recommendation is that you take one or two bottles of ginseng a day, which I did. My policy is to take both vitamin supplements and ginseng on a regular basis, but then a week or two before an important competition I build up, taking quite a lot more on the theory that competition takes a lot more out of you in emotional terms than training.

At Nihon I followed that policy, and when I arrived in Seoul I was told that the Korean ginseng also had very good qualities.

These were in tablet form. I still continued with my liquid, however, because I am quite a big person, much bigger than average, so when the recommended dose is, say, four tablets for the average person, I would take six or eight. Before the 100 metres final I took two bottles down to the track and drank them quite openly. Now, before the 200 metres, because I was tired, because I was tackling four rounds of double the distance and because I didn't want to carry them all the way back home, I decided to drink everything I had left on the night before and the day of the final.

The 200 metres has been something of a bogey event for me. In Stuttgart I had been eliminated at the semi-final stage, and I hadn't even been able to compete in the event in Edinburgh and Rome because of injury. Even this year in Budapest I had only come third in the European Indoor. It was only in 1988 that my times began to reach respectability. Now, in Seoul, I had a great chance to graduate at 200 metres. I had run a windy 20.37 seconds and had beaten John Regis (all but once) and the Frenchman Queneherve, both of them World Championship medallists behind Calvin Smith. Calvin wasn't there, so I thought I was in with a chance.

The first-round heats were mid-morning on the second Monday of the Games. This necessitated another early morning rise. I am not normally a crack-of-dawn riser to say the least, and my only consolation was that for Ron and everyone watching back in Britain it was 2 a.m. I was in the seventh heat of ten. Ahead of me both Michael Rosswess and John Regis had qualified easily, and I did likewise ahead of Bruno Marie-Rose. For the faster men these opening-round heats were no more than leg-stretchers.

Three hours later we were back in the stadium for the next round. The likely finalists should emerge at this stage, and they did so. Carl won the opening race ahead of John Regis; Marie-Rose beat the American Roy Martin, Joe De Loach won and Robson da Silva, the Brazilian, ran the niftiest heat of the day in 20.41 seconds. I won my heat, again easing down slowly, beating Atlee Mahorn of Canada. It was the third-fastest time and I was pleased. Young Michael had also progressed, so we had three Britons in the semi-finals. There was now another day's rest before those races and the final.

This gave me a chance to go out and do some supporting. Colin had reached the final of the 110 metres hurdles, and Jon Ridgeon and Tony Jarrett were there with him. He had run well in the opening rounds but in the semi had only come third. The main obstacle between Colin and gold was the defending champion, Roger Kingdom. A whole crowd of us roared ourselves hoarse during that final. Kingdom won, but Colin came through magnificently to take the silver medal. The Union Jacks waved in the stadium again and I felt almost as happy and proud as when I had run my European record.

Our section on the top floor had done particularly well, in fact. David Ottley had reached the final of the javelin with a personal best throw – not bad in your last Olympics; Dalton Grant had been magnificent in the high jump, setting a new British record of 2.31 metres and coming seventh in the final; and Colin and I had our medals. (Dalton also won the sleeping competition hands down. I've never seen anybody sleep as much as he did; it was as if he was on night-shift!)

Great Britain had had an up-and-down Olympics so far. Apart from Linford and Colin Jackson, Yvonne Murray had gained a bronze in the 3000 metres with the bravest run of her life. Fatima Whitbread, after giving her British supporters palpitations in the qualifying round, took the silver medal in the javelin. Kriss Akabussi, despite his injury problems, reached the final of the 400 metres hurdles and finished sixth in a race that finally saw the end of the reign of Edwin Moses. But in the distance events, so long the flagship of British athletics, disaster had struck when, in the 800 metres, first Tom McKean had been disqualified for blatant barging in his second-round heat and then Steve Cram had been lifeless at the crucial stage of his race and come home sixth to be a non-qualifier. It was left to Peter Elliott, who was receiving daily cortisone injections for a groin injury, to salvage some of the British reputation with a fighting fourth in the final. In these Games the glory was to be taken by the sprinters and hurdlers.

Flo-Jo had won the 100 metres in devastating style, silencing the sceptics with a new Olympic record of 10.54 seconds. Her sister-in-law had also set a new world record in the heptathlon.

Now the Olympic Stadium was to have time to catch its breath from all the excitement, as the second Tuesday of the Games was designated the athletics rest day. The previous evening, Linford and his friends decided to raid the great kerb market of Itaewan in downtown Seoul. In the Land of the Morning Calm, this street was like bedlam.

Itaewan was an extraordinary place, and I had never seen anything like it before. We went there by taxi. The taxis in Seoul were quite a feature of the Olympics: smiling Koreans in white gloves, with a smattering of English, would drive you miles and miles for what appeared to be very little recompense. The twelve-mile journey from the Village to Itaewan cost around £4, approximately the fare from Victoria to Paddington in London.

Both sides of the streets were lined with stalls selling everything you could think of, including vast quantities of white socks. They were piled high on each booth, stamped Nike, Yves St Laurent, Fila – every fashionable logo the producers could think of. Korea, and particularly Itaewan, is the world headquarters of fake designer merchandise. From Reebok trainers to Rolex watches, there was a huge selection at a tenth of the price of the legitimate product, and you would be hard pressed to recognize the difference (although of course, you didn't have the guarantees!). As we walked along, attempts would be made to entice us into tailors, where made-to-measure suits could be turned out in three days, or into shoe shops, where the same standard applied. It was, of course, a great magnet for everyone visiting the Olympics. I guarantee that if you had stood in the middle of Itaewan for the duration of the Games you would have met every visiting athlete there. We all indulged ourselves that night, like children let loose in an ice-cream factory. I was measured for a suit, and Colin got heavily into the leather goods. We went back a few times but in the end the crowds got me down, as well as the pushing, shoving and haggling that seemed to accompany every purchase. After our first visit there we returned to the Village quite late, secure in the knowledge that we could all have a lie-in the next morning.

15
Shock

The insistent telephone ring finally broke through my unconsciousness. It was still dark. I padded across the floor of the flat in Olympic Town, picked up the receiver and said 'Hello' a little huskily.

'Hello, Tone,' said a familiar voice, 'it's Jim Rosenthal.'

'Jesus, Jim,' I said, 'what time is it?'

It's five-fifteen,' he replied. 'Sorry to ring you so early, but Ben Johnson has been done for taking drugs.'

I was totally incredulous. 'Oh come on, Jim,' I said. 'What kind of gag is this for this time of the morning?'

'No gag at all,' he said. 'I'm afraid it's true, horribly true. The IOC Executive will announce it later today.' He sounded deadly serious, totally sincere. By now I was wide awake, the implications of what he was saying whizzing through my mind. I said, 'My God!'

'Yes,' said Jim. 'Look, we would really like to talk to Linford.'

'Not now, surely?'

'No, no,' he said hastily. 'Later on – say around eight o'clock.'

'Well, I'll try,' I said, 'but I can't promise. I'll have to get up to the Village.'

'Of course,' he said. 'Will you phone me from there?'

'Yes,' I replied. 'Jim, this is awful.'

'You're dead right, mate,' he said, and rang off.

I dressed quickly, grabbed my Cellnet telephone and headed for the taxi rank outside the campus gates. 'Olympic Village?' asked the driver. I nodded. It was about three miles from the Olympic Town to the Village. I couldn't get my thoughts together; I was too stunned at the news. We drove past the enormous Kajyale Market, whose fish and vegetable vendors were already out haggling over prices, but I hardly took in the scene – my thoughts were elsewhere.

The guards smiled and saluted as I went through the last security *check. The British headquarters was wreathed in darkness. I awoke Les Jones, whose room was adjacent to the front door. He came out fighting off sleep and then stared in disbelief when I told him the news. We decided to ring around and try to get confirmation. It was difficult to obtain; people were either not answering calls or being evasive. We did learn, however, that the IAAF President, the urbane Italian Primo Nebiolo, had quietly informed his Council colleagues at a function the previous evening that he had to call a meeting that morning to discuss a matter 'of grave importance'. This seemed a clinching piece of information. I re-contacted Jim Rosenthal, who said that the International Olympic Committee had called a press conference for ten o'clock. I agreed that we would wake Linford at eight o'clock to see if he would appear on television.*

Tony and Les Jones woke me up. They told me that Ben had been found positive on his drug test. I didn't believe them at first; neither did Colin. Gradually, however, I realized that this wasn't some premature April fool joke but was horribly true. I reluctantly agreed to go on television, though I wish I had been protected from that. I talked to both ITV and BBC, who had permanent cameras installed in the British Olympic headquarters. All I could say was that I was sorry for Ben, that he was a good friend of mine. I was in a state of shock.

When the pictures were being shown in Britain, many people noticed that I was looking down all the time the interview was taking place. They thought that I was either embarrassed or emotionally cut up. What I was actually doing was looking at the monitor that was on the floor. I was taken aback that there was neither a cameraman nor an interviewer there, just a camera pointing at me. I was actually talking to people in London.

Later in the day I met one of the Canadian sprint coaches. Their team was, of course, traumatized. 'I'm really sorry to hear about Ben,' I said to him, and then suddenly the tears came, I couldn't hold them back. I cried for Ben because I felt so sorry for him. I have always argued that anyone who is found positive should be banned for life, but you always hope that it's not going to happen to someone you know. I cried because it hurt. It was a sad, sad day. I wasn't crying only for Ben Johnson, I was crying for my sport. I love my athletics. It is the vehicle that has enabled me to express myself, it is the only thing that I have ever been really good at – I was never going to be a world-class scholar or musician or anything. Sprinting has given me self-respect, taken me out the ruck. It is my business. And now, I thought, it is the end of athletics as we know it.

At ten o'clock the IOC called its press conference. A substance had been found in the sample given by the sprinter Ben Johnson, namely 'stanozol, an anabolic steroid'. The statement continued:

'The IOC Medical Commission discussed all arguments presented by the Canadian Delegation, especially the statement that the substance in question might have been administered after the competition by a third party. The steroid profile, however, is not consistent with such a claim. The IOC Medical Commission recommends the following sanction: disqualification of this competitor from the Games. The decision is unanimous. No right of appeal is given.'

Fifty minutes later Ben Johnson, his family and his coach Charlie Francis were boarding, amid scenes of noisy pandemonium, a Korean Airlines flight from Kimpo to New York.

Collectively we had always got on well with the Canadians. They are a happy-go-lucky crowd, anxious to win like everybody else but never, unlike the Americans, giving themselves superior airs and graces or taking their competitiveness outside the tracks. Ben and I had discussed sprinting; Mark McCoy had helped Colin with hurdling. Now they were a team in disgrace, shattered beyond belief. The 100 metres hadn't been just a sporting event, it had been *news*. Millions of people around the world who normally had no interest in track and field had been lured by the drama of it. After the race Ben had spoken to the Canadian Prime Minister live on television, and the Premier had said that every Canadian had been made proud that day. In Jamaica people had celebrated in the streets. All of this served only to heighten the fall when it came.

Of course, there had been rumours about Ben. After the World Championships in Rome Carl had gone on television before the meeting had ended and given out a lot of innuendo, indirectly implicating Ben in drug-taking. But there are rumours about everybody – about me, about Colin, about anybody who manages to beat the Americans. As Gran used to say, 'Thieves think that everybody steals.' I shouldn't be surprised if some of the people who shout the loudest about drug-taking may in fact be found to be indulging themselves.

As the day progressed, so the story unfolded. Undoubtedly there had been a massive leak from the IOC test laboratories. Millions around the world knew about Ben Johnson's positive test well before most people in Seoul. Rumours about bribery of the Korean lab technicians were rife.

It was late on the Sunday night, the day after the 100 metres final, that the IOC Committee was told that the first test of Johnson's sample had shown positive for an anabolic steroid. At 1.45 a.m. on the Monday, the Canadian Olympic Association was informed. They in turn told Charlie Francis, who went to the Hilton Hotel to break the news to his athlete. Subsequently Francis's heavy involvement in his athletes' drug-taking would be revealed, so who knows what words were exchanged between them? Later that day the Canadians attended the IOC laboratories for the second test of Ben's B sample, the back-up to the original. It again showed positive. The IOC Medical Commission met and decided that Johnson should be banned; their Executive concurred. In the middle of Tuesday night, Ben was stripped of his Olympic gold medal. The IAAF announced that he was automatically banned for two years, and that his world record of 9.79 seconds would not be recognized.

Throughout that Tuesday people were simply stunned by what had happened, found it difficult to come to terms with. Linford now had the silver medal, Calvin Smith was promoted to the bronze. In Canada Ben had been clapped and cheered on his arrival at Toronto airport, and another crowd had gathered outside his home. He arrived but could not get in because he did not have his key, so he was left standing on his own doorstep, the crowd watching, the television cameras filming. It seemed to sum up the whole situation. Now everyone knew what the Games of the XXIVth Olympiad would be remembered for.

Thoughts of Ben stayed with me all that day, mainly of the disgrace of it all and, because of that, how he must be feeling. I was glad in the end that it had been announced when it had, when there were no events taking place, because if there had been they would undoubtedly have suffered from all the adverse publicity.

Life must go on though, and we received the draw for the semi-finals of the 200 metres. I was running against Joe De Loach, one of the favourites, and Mike Rosswess, but all in all it was not a difficult heat. John Regis was drawn in the first race, a much tougher one, against Carl, Robson da Silva, Atlee Mahorn and Queneherve, and he had also received a bad draw with the inside lane. Our team management made some sort of protest but to no avail, and John brooded about his draw all that afternoon and evening. I had some sympathy with him – I had been in exactly the same situation at the European Indoor and had moped and protested. But this is counter-productive; in the end the only thing you can do is to put it out of your mind and go out and do the business. John didn't do that, and he ran badly the next day.

De Loach was a tough competitor. He was a training companion and friend of Carl, and had beaten him at the US Olympic Trials. He had a best time of 19.96 seconds. Furthermore, he was coming fresh to the event; he hadn't competed in the 100 metres. Joe ran really hard and clocked 20.06 seconds, by far the fastest time of the event so far. I just ran a relaxed race in order to qualify. Carl had won the first semi. The big surprise was Rosswess running fourth in my heat and getting to the final; it was only his second year in serious athletics. I saw him at the warm-up track afterwards and he was in a total daze. I was beginning to feel sore, to ache after all the racing I had been doing. I had never before run so many races in such a short time span, and I was glad I had taken all of my ginseng.

I thought that the final was a very open race. I was feeling very confident after the 100 metres and I really wanted to do well in this 200. It was the fifth day of the athletics events and a gold medal was proving elusive for the British athletes. Colin and Fatima, and now I (though I actually thought by default) all had silver medals. But no one had captured what Daley calls the 'Big G'. Our supporters in Seoul were really marvellous – cheering, waving huge Union Jacks, calling out our names – and my heart went out to them. I wanted to give them something to shout about, to be able to grab that Union Jack and run around the track and hear the cheering, to let everyone know that the Brits were there.

I had a good draw, with De Loach outside me. I thought that the best plan was to catch him as quickly as possible and then hold on to my lead down the straight. It was a good plan except that, in the race, I didn't catch him! It wasn't until afterwards that I learned he had a best time for the 100 metres of 10.03. I held the bronze-medal position until the last few strides of the race and then the Brazilian Robson da Silva came past. I set a new British record of 20.09 seconds as a consolation prize for fourth, also becoming the third-fastest ever European. De Loach beat Carl, 19.76 to 19.79 seconds for a new Olympic record.

Looking back on the Olympics, I don't think that I had done enough real work to break through the 20-seconds barrier. It is becoming obvious that the race is getting to be more specialist. Carl is finding that, too; gone are the days when he can achieve what he did in Los Angeles. Then he was in a league of his own, but now there is much sterner opposition from all parts of the world. Only three of us in that final were also in the 100 metres final, and there is no doubt that da Silva is more of a 200 metres specialist. Carl had already won the long jump gold medal, but without Ben's positive drug test that would have been the only one he would have achieved.

Michael Rosswess's performance mirrored exactly that of Ade Mafe in 1984. His is obviously a marvellous talent but already, during the 1989 indoor season, he is being boosted by both television and the press as the great future hope just as Ade was. He must learn from Ade's experiences, learn, as the poem says, to deal with both triumph and disaster. His is a talent that needs nurturing, not exploiting in the way that Ade's was.

After 1986 Ade sustained some injuries and lost form. He had over-committed himself financially and went through a very rough time indeed. I don't think that he received either the right coaching or the right advice. He simply became caught up in all the media hype that at one time surrounded him. In 1988 he reappeared at West London Stadium, training on his own, and after the Olympics with Ron's agreement I asked him if he would like to join us in the squad. He has had some notable indoor success, and I'm also pleased, as the elder statesman of the sprinters, that he is around at the same time as Michael, as a salutary reminder, if Michael needs one, of what can happen.

After the 200 metres I felt even more stiff and sore. I had run eight races in six days and still had the relays to come. After I collected my gear, I found that I had been selected for a drug test, along with the three medal winners. During the Thursday, the day after the 200 metres when I was not competing, I was walking around in a new tee-shirt to go with my 'Pure Talent' one. It said 'Drug Free Zone'. A reporter asked me, 'Well, what do you think should happen to those people caught taking drugs?'

I said, 'They should be banned for life. No reprieve.'

They were words that I would well remember come the next day.

16
Bitter Tears

I had had a relaxed, easy day and was feeling in good spirits. A whole gang of us had been to the Village restaurant for dinner and a lively argument had developed about patriotism, which continued as we left to cross the road back towards the British apartment block. On the way we met Mike Turner, the team manager, who had apparently been looking for me. He said, 'Linford, can I have a word with you?' We moved to one side while the rest of the group, now giggling a little, went on.

Mike Turner had been the team manager since 1985 and had been with us through Stuttgart, Rome and numerous European and World Indoor meetings and a host of internationals. He is a nice, kindly man, but not my idea of a dynamic leader. He is, in 'real life', a Cambridge don. He is also Mr Patriotism himself and I thought that he had overheard our argument and was about to deliver an erudite lecture on the subject. Instead he said, 'We've had a letter from the IOC to say that they have found an illegal substance in your test sample.'

I gaped at him and then laughed. 'Get out of here!' I said. I thought that he was out for some fun. 'You're joking!'

'I can assure you,' he said, 'that I have never been more serious in my life.'

I still didn't believe him, thinking that here was some elaborate hoax. Then I looked at his face. He was deadly serious. 'No. Oh no! There must be some mistake,' I told him, but I could see that there wasn't.

The first thought that flashed through my mind was that Ben had said that his sample must have been sabotaged in doping control. I thought that there must be a conspiracy going on. I said, 'Sabotage! Somebody out there is jealous and has sabotaged

With Tessa Sanderson at Heathrow prior to flying to Seoul – this triggered off a *News of the World* fairy tale

With John Herbert and John Regis receiving Budget Rental Cars from the British Olympic Association before Seoul in 1988

First race in a double sprint win at the AAA Championships in 1988 – the first since 1953 – when I won the 100 metres . . .

. . . and the second when I beat John Regis in the 200 metres. The championships were also the Olympic Trials

The relay final in Seoul and I'm away on one of the fastest 'legs' of all time to give Great Britain the silver medal

My two Olympic silver medals

A wonderful moment when I am made a Freeman of the Boroughs of Hammersmith and Fulham. I give Mum a kiss to thank her for everything

Daley Thompson commiserates with me after just missing a medal in the Olympic 200 metres. Training with the great man in the winter of 1987–88 set me up for my Olympic medals

On the way to Barcelona. I start the next Olympiad at the AAA Indoor Championships at Cosford.

my sample like they did to Ben. If they want my medal they can have it. But don't tell me that I'm on drugs.' I did not know whether to laugh or to cry, I was in such a state of shock. Then I cried. I didn't know where I was or what was happening. I kept moaning, 'No, no, no'.

We walked back to the athletes' apartment block. By this time I was beginning to feel a little hysterical. I thought about the shame of it all, what the world would say. I thought about my new tee-shirt, 'Drug Free Zone'. The letter from the IOC Medical Commission did not indicate what the substance was but with the prevailing atmosphere after Ben's positive test, the natural reaction was steroids. And that is what I thought: 'My God, they've found steroids!'

We assembled in the downstairs room that served as an office. I was faced by Mike Turner, Ewan Murray, the Chairman of the British Board, and Malcolm Read, the team doctor. I think his assistant, Malcolm Bottomley, joined us later. I had to relay to them everything that I had done and eaten both on the day of the test – which was taken after the 200 metres – and on the day before that. I was grilled; there is no other word for it. I felt that I wasn't being believed. They were making me feel like a criminal. It indicated how everyone had been affected by the Ben Johnson affair, how easy it would have been to start a witch hunt. I kept repeating everything. It was a real cross-examination.

At one time I had to leave the meeting. I said to myself, 'You've done it. Somehow, you've done it.' I had got to the stage where I myself believed that somehow I had taken steroids, and was on the point of admitting that I was on hard drugs. I now understand how innocent people under intense interrogation admit to crimes they have not committed, and how after they have been interviewed, women can feel guilty when they have been raped. I used to be sceptical about that, but not any more. Maybe they were just making absolutely sure in their own minds whether or not I had taken anything. I don't know, but in the end I broke down.

I cried. I was shaking. I hadn't cried so much or so bitterly since my granny had died. I thought that my whole world was about to fall apart. I thought of Ron, who had stayed out on that cold track all winter in all weathers and taken time off work without pay to come and see me train. And I thought, by calling me a cheat they are calling my coach a cheat. They are calling the people I train with cheats. At this time, of course, we still had no idea what the 'substance' was to which the IOC were referring.

I went into the next block to repeat my explanations to the British Olympic Association. On the way across I met Daley, returning battered and bruised from his decathlon in which he had just failed to win a medal. He looked at me, and said, 'You're in trouble, aren't you?' Apparently some rumours were already circulating in the stadium.

I told him what had happened. 'Daley,' I asked, 'do you believe that I'm on drugs?'

'No chance,' he said. It made me feel a little better.

Next it transpired that two British team members had had positive tests. The other was the judo competitor, Kerrith Brown, who had won a bronze medal. The whole thing was evolving into a ghastly nightmare. I went upstairs to our room. My first instincts had been to tell the team and certainly the group that I was going around with. I trusted them implicitly and in any case I wanted no whispering campaigns. But I was told not to tell anybody. Frankly, it was an impossible request in such circumstances. Dalton was the only person in our section. I tried to act in a casual manner but I badly needed to talk to somebody, so I embarked upon a very convoluted conversation.

'Dalton,' I said, 'if you were in my position, earning the money that I'm earning, would you go on drugs?'

'No way,' replied Dalton. 'If I was in your position I wouldn't need to.'

'Has it ever crossed your mind that I'm on drugs?' I persisted.

'No.'

'The BOA have just told me that there was a substance in my urine.'

'No, not you,' said Dalton, 'not you.'

I told him to keep it to himself. When Colin came in I told him everything.

'Get over, man,' he said in his lilting Welsh accent.

'It's true,' I said.

Colin began to laugh and then stopped, realizing how serious I was. He just shook his head in disbelief. Malcolm Arnold joined us and I could tell by the way they were reacting that they thought, as I had done in the beginning, that this was some enormous hoax being set up. I sounded a little angry. 'Look, I'm serious,' I said.

'If you're on drugs,' said Colin, 'I'm on drugs.' He said that because we both take exactly the same dietary supplements – with the exception of ginseng.

My mind dwelt on the shame of it all, not only for me but for my family, my coach, my friends. And when I thought about my Mum and Dad sitting comfortably at home, oblivious to all this, so proud of what I had achieved, it made me even more distraught. I began to feel suicidal, and kept trying to climb over the ninth-floor balcony. In the end, in the middle of the night, Malcolm Read gave me some sleeping tablets to try to help me calm down and sleep. I slept fitfully.

Early that morning a contingent from the British Olympic Association drove to the IOC medical laboratories in Seoul. Encamped outside the building since the Johnson affair had broken were the media – television and press. Among the BOA group was the BOA Secretary Dick Palmer, the judo team manager Arthur Mapp, and Mike Turner. There were also medical representatives of both sports, Malcolm Read for athletics and Kenneth Kingsbury for judo.

As they climbed from their car so the media members stirred, the cameras rolled and the rumours that had already been circulating were confirmed: a British athlete and a judo competitor had been found positive. That news was instantly flashed around the world. The BOA people went inside for the second tests on both men's B samples. They confirmed the positive result.

Malcolm Read came to see me and explained that they now knew what the substance was: pseudoephedrine, a stimulant that is normally found in cough linctus and other medicines. He said that they had found eight parts in a million, and I found out later that if that amount had appeared in a test in Britain it would have been ignored. Now that the team management knew what the substance was, a whole new line of questioning began. What did I take? Had I taken any cough medicines? I had to produce all my cartons of vitamins and ginseng.

I went back to the BOA offices to meet Robert Watson, who in addition to being the Treasurer of the British Olympic Association is also a Queen's Counsel. He was the man who was going to lead the defence at the hearing that evening. Watson is okay; if I were being tried for my life I'd like to have him on my side. On this Friday morning, though, I was in such a state that I didn't want to trust anybody. He said, 'I think when we get to the Enquiry we'll say that you've been taking some cough medicine and they'll give you a little slap on the wrist and that will be it.'

'No,' I replied. 'I don't take any cough medicine. Why should I take a rap for taking cough medicine when I haven't taken any, never take any?'

He looked at me long and hard. 'I believe you,' he said suddenly. 'I said that because I wanted to find out whether you would accept it. It was a test. I believe that you haven't knowingly taken anything.'

I felt some relief. Clearly, if Watson was going out to defend me it was imperative that he believe I was innocent.

I travelled down to the stadium, as I was due to run in the heats of the relay that morning. When I arrived I began to tell everyone I knew, as quietly as I could, what was happening. Already rumours were rife, and outside the warm-up track the press and television reporters were gathered in droves. I had told Tessa the previous night, and now I spoke to Pam and Joan, Daley and Greg Richards, another decathlete, Frank Dick, and other members of my group. Mike Turner had told me to keep quiet until after the Enquiry, but I just couldn't. I badly needed all the support that I could get. The problem was that every time I tried to explain what was going on I began to cry – it was uncontrollable.

I could see that everyone felt for me. I wasn't sure whether or not they believed that I had knowingly taken a stimulant, and I had to get it out of my system. I looked people straight in the eye and asked, 'Do you believe it?' They said no, and I believed them. Of course, I was still nevertheless distraught.

Frank Dick was highly supportive and helpful. He seemed genuinely concerned, even though we had been feuding all these years, been at each other's throats like schoolboys. We decided that I should warm up with the relay team, but we also decided that I shouldn't run in the first-round heats. 'Maybe it's best if you don't run,' Frank said. 'You won't be able to concentrate and the anxiety you're feeling could transmit itself and cause an injury. Carry on as normal, warm up and then we'll announce that you've sustained a niggle as a result of the 200 metres.' I agreed with that. There was also the consideration that if I was banned in the evening, the whole team would be disqualified.

The story broke mid-morning via Independent Television. There are many and varied explanations as to how they got to know, but by this time more and more people in the team had been told. Again, millions in Britain knew before a lot of people in Seoul. A great gloom had settled over the British camp and the team members and managers were being accosted by the press every time they left the warm-up track. ITV had a camera high above the warm-up area and all morning it had been pointing in towards the small tent that served as an ad hoc headquarters.

By now the doctors, Read and Bottomley, were homing in on the ginseng as a likely source of the pseudoephedrine.

I went out to watch the relay heats and to cheer on the team from the competitors' section of the grandstand. I was trying hard to keep cheerful and to keep it from my mind, but of course it was impossible. The team qualified by running second in the final heat behind Hungary. John Regis moved to the second leg and Clarence Callender ran the anchor. The USA actually won the race but after protests were disqualified for a faulty change-over. They had been having their team difficulties too; in Nihon it had been rumoured that the coaches wanted to keep Carl off the team.

As I was leaving the stand Jim Rosenthal came up and asked if I would give ITV an interview. I said that I would love to but I had been told to say nothing until after the Enquiry. I thought it was best to stick with that. Jim was understanding, as he always is, and when I came back to Britain and looked at the videos and read all the papers I saw that, for once, everyone had been extremely supportive. One journalist told me that he had written, 'Saying that Linford Christie is on drugs is like saying the Pope is an adulterer,' but that his paper had, wisely perhaps, refused to print it! Nor had I realized the tremendous public support that was welling up, especially when it transpired that steroids were not involved and the amount of pseudoephedrine that was being talked about was so small.

When we returned to the Village in the afternoon there were two developments. The test results revealed that, of Kerrith's and my samples, one was a serious case and the other not so serious, and apparently the judo people were not being very forthcoming about what was contained in his sample, so our people were somewhat in the dark. The other development was that ginseng was now the prime suspect in my particular case, and I had to produce all my bottles and tablets.

I spoke to Anna-Lisa Hammer on the telephone. She had arrived in Seoul but had been unable to gain access to the Village. Since I had last seen her she had been investigating the drug scene and had written a book about David Jenkins, the former British 400 metres record holder who went to jail in California for drug-dealing, principally steroids, in Mexico and the USA. She told me about American athletes in the US Trials who had been tested positive for pseudoephedrine. The amounts involved were much higher than mine, but explanations about the runners taking cough medicine had been accepted.

In the evening we set off for the Hotel Shilla in Seoul for the Enquiry, leaving the Village by a back entrance in a number of cars. We were quite a large contingent: the judo people, members of the athletics team management and, of course, the BOA. When the convoy arrived at the hotel there was absolute bedlam – TV camera crews, microphones, glaring lights, pressmen, people shouting questions, utter pandemonium. I had seen television pictures of Ben leaving the airport, pushing his way through a great throng of people, and this was just as bad. It was also absolutely scandalous. This was supposed to be a private enquiry, and yet here it was being held in the full glare of world publicity. Even though the Princess Royal, as a member of the International Committee, was staying at the hotel, security seemed to have gone out of the window.

We pushed and shoved our way towards the lift, ignoring all the questions being fired at us. A cameraman entered the lift, his lighting man with him, and tried to start filming. I spoke for the first time. 'If you value your life,' I said, 'don't poke that thing in my face.' They tried to follow us out into the corridor but were quickly dissuaded. I was seething. It seemed to me that catching Ben had gone to the IOC's collective head and that all they were after were scapegoats and publicity for their fight against drugs.

We sat in a small bedroom and discussed the procedures. I knew by now that Kerrith Brown was in much greater trouble than I was. Robert Watson is an outspoken man who doesn't mince his words, and he said simply that Brown had been damned stupid. Kerrith went down first to face the IOC Medical Committee and, as it turned out, the music. They found him guilty and took away his bronze medal. It was a sad day for British judo, and an even sadder day for him. To me, sitting in the bedroom on the top floor of the Shilla, Kerrith's proceedings seemed to take a lifetime. Finally I was summoned down to face the Enquiry.

The hotel corridor which led to the room where the Drug Enquiry was being held was bursting at the seams with pressmen and women, all eagerly anticipating a new arrival. There was literally no clear way through the vast mêlée, with media men constantly shouting, shoving and trying to attain the best positions to face Linford and the BOA entourage. It was quite extraordinary that the International Olympic Committee had chosen this very public place for the Enquiry. They seemed hell-bent, officially or unofficially, on obtaining maximum publicity for their activities.

There was a growing opinion in Seoul that the IOC felt that they were the lone crusaders against drug abuse, that the international sporting federations were not wholehearted in their battles with the drug-takers. Following the scandal of the Italian officials in Rome trying to cheat their long jumper Giovanni Evangelisti into the bronze medal, and given Primo Nebiolo's lukewarm attitude towards stiffer legislation against drug abusers, IOC members were questioning whether, under the IAAF, Ben Johnson would have been exposed.

The heat in the corridor was intense under the television lights as Linford arrived to stand before the Enquiry, under the Chairmanship of Prince Alexandre de Marode.

It was totally disgusting. I seemed to have no control over my own movements, to be simply carried along by the throng, battered, pushed and jolted, cameras in my face, the heat and glare of the lights making me sweat, microphones under my nose, people shouting and bawling questions. It felt as if I was taking part in a TV court-room drama. I grabbed one microphone and dragged it along in the hope that its owner would get into the Enquiry. I knew that I had done nothing wrong. I held my head high and made no comment.

The Enquiry room reminded me of the European Court in Strasbourg – big tables and microphones everywhere. The room was set in a square, and we were to sit at one end. Robert Watson presented my case, and I was even more impressed with him. As he expounded our viewpoint he reminded me of a television lawyer. It was the second time in a few minutes that I had had this sense that I was part of a fictitious drama.

Prince de Marode then asked me if I had anything to say. Every time he spoke there was a delay because he insisted on speaking in French, even though he could speak English fairly well, so his words had to be translated.

'Sirs,' I said, 'I have always been an outspoken person on drug abuse; I have always been willing to campaign against drugs. I have never even taken an aspirin in my life. The only things that I have ever taken are in front of you.' Lined up in front were samples of all my vitamin supplements and ginseng, which they then began to pass around. 'I would never,' I concluded, 'take any illegal substances ever.'

The questioning was then thrown open to the members of the Medical Commission. Where did I buy my vitamins? Where did I obtain my ginseng? I was gaining the distinct impression that some of the Commission considered the proceedings a complete waste of time but that others, the hard-liners, were determined to pursue it to the bitter end.

I told them that I hadn't changed my routine at all since arriving in Japan and Korea except for finishing off all my ginseng. 'Why did you take such large quantities?' one of the Committee asked. 'Did you think it would enhance your performance?'

'I do not take anything to enhance my performance,' I replied. 'I take these supplements and ginseng for my whole well-being. I take them because I put my body through a tremendous stress and strain, which is unnatural. I think it is important to take vitamins in larger volume than a normal person.'

'Why did you take larger quantities of ginseng before the 200 metres?'

'Because,' I replied, 'it is a longer distance, double the distance of my main race, so I felt that I needed to replace energy quickly. I also wanted to get rid of it all to avoid carrying it back to Britain.'

It was over. We adjourned to a small adjacent room. I thought about the Enquiry and the questions, but there was no way of telling how it had gone. There seemed to be mixed reactions. I felt there were some people there who looked upon drug abuse as just one symptom of the degeneration of the sport they had once taken part in and loved, that drugs, money, publicity, and individual success had finally dragged it down, and they were out for blood. Others, I thought, were looking upon the whole thing as a wasted evening.

We sat in the room for about ten minutes and then returned to the Enquiry. There were further exchanges and then Robert Watson said, 'Let's go,' and we left. There was no verdict; nobody said a word to me. Robert told me to go back to the Village and get some sleep.

The press and the television reporters stayed on, still filling the corridor outside the Enquiry room. After a while Prince de Marode appeared in his shirt-sleeves, firstly to tell the journalists that nothing would be said until the official statement was released, and then, suddenly, under a barrage of questions, announcing that Linford had been cleared to run in the relay the next day. He had, said the Belgian Prince, been given 'the benefit of the doubt'. Later the BOA Press Officer, Caroline Searle, issued a statement concerning both Kerrith Brown and Linford. The British media (with the possible exception of the Sun newspaper), the British public and, not least, Linford heaved a collective sigh of relief.

I went back to the Village, back to my room. Much later in the small hours, Malcolm Read came up to tell me that everything was fine, that I was cleared to run pending the approval of the IOC Executive, which was a formality. I had never experienced a greater feeling of relief than when I heard Malcolm's words. For me it was tantamount to having been on Death Row and reprieved at the eleventh hour. I would not wish a similar twenty-four hours on my worst enemy.

Later, of course, came the anger. Firstly, nobody from the IOC has ever officially given me the verdict of the Enquiry. All the information I received on the subject was at second hand. Secondly, there were the words 'benefit of the doubt'. I feel, and have said so, that I am owed an apology for those words. What do they mean? They cast a slur, of course, and they would never be used in English law; you are either guilty or not guilty. But despite an exchange of lawyers' letters I have not received an apology from the Prince de Marode.

Some excuses were made for the Prince on the basis that his English had let him down. I found that interesting. During the Enquiry he had insisted on speaking in French, presumably because he wanted to ensure that his meaning would be completely clear. If he was, therefore, so unsure of his English, why did he insist on going out to meet the world's media? Why did he not leave it to the official statement or let somebody whose command of English was better do the job for the Enquiry? I don't know if these questions have ever been asked. All I know is that they certainly haven't been answered. Nor has anyone ever explained how the voting on the Enquiry, that it was not a unanimous decision, became known to the press.

I do not know under what law we were operating in Seoul. I was however, extremely grateful that the IAAF supported my feelings. John Holt, its General Secretary, was also angered by de Marode's remarks, and Arne Lundqvist, an IAAF member, told me that he thought the fuss over my test had been a complete waste of time. 'For that amount,' he said, 'there should have been no reporting, no second testing.'

Colin was happy; in fact, everyone was delighted. It was as if a black cloud overhanging the team had lifted and a warm sun come shining through. It had been the very worst day of my life. I settled down to sleep, and did so very well. Tomorrow was the final day of the Olympic Games, and we had the relay still to come.

The implications of the manner of drug testing at the 1988 Olympic Games and the attendant publicity were still being discussed many months later. A number of individuals and organizations were indicating that it must never happen again.

There were constant leakages from the laboratories of the IOC Medical Commission throughout the weeks that it was operating, and it seemed that little was being done to prevent it. The International Olympic Committee appeared to be revelling in its self-appointed role as the guardian of the integrity of world sport and taking advantage of global attention, focused on Seoul, to ram the message home. The Ben Johnson case was handled absolutely correctly, despite a leak to the media, with the testing of the A and B samples and the subsequent official announcement. Linford's case was handled in a much greater glare of publicity. The fact that his first test was suspect was known to a very large group of people, including journalists and television commentators, before the second test was carried out. Indeed, it seems likely that people at the Olympic Stadium knew on the Thursday evening, before Linford did. The venue and time of the subsequent Enquiry also became known to the media, which once again smacked of publicity-seeking. Worst of all, the Medical Commission and the IOC seemed to display an arrogant lack of sensitivity to the human consequences of their actions and to the torment suffered by the innocent as well as the guilty because of the manner in which they carried out their procedures.

One of the salient questions to be asked is why the IOC felt it necessary to rush through their procedures as they did, so that the guilty might be punished before the Games were over. The business of the clandestine delivery of letters from Medical Commission to Olympic Associations very late at night and the subsequent all-night discussions, the early morning journeys for the second tests, further late-night enquiries and early morning announcements all pointed to people operating with one eye on prime-time television. Many people felt that it had more than faint undertones of the trials of the witches of Salem and, in more modern times, of the McCarthy hearings in the United States in the early 1950s. Many asked if anti-drug zealots were in control of the authorities.

I woke up on the Saturday morning raring to go. Our semi-final was at midday and we arrived at the warm-up track in good time. It was quickly decided that I should run the last leg. As my granny frequently used to say, the hand of God works in mysterious ways! It was, as always, Frank Dick's decision. He said that it was not worth changing the team around at this stage so I would be slipped in on the end. It suited me just fine. Nevertheless I was very tired through stress and lack of sleep, and spent most of the morning yawning away.

I had now, quietly, received my silver medal from Carl. There had been some talk of re-staging the 100 metres medal ceremony, but in the end the idea was scrapped and I was glad about that. I was loath to give up my bronze medal; it was the one that I had won, the one that had been presented to me. In the end, however, I surrendered it to Calvin Smith.

There was always the chance that all the stress I had been subjected to might transmit itself physically and that I would pull my hamstring, so I warmed up particularly carefully and had a long massage.

We knew that we were in with a chance of a medal in the relay now that the United States team had been disqualified. It had taken quite a lot of protesting to achieve this. The Korean change-over judges had signalled a white flag indicating a fair exchange on the final take-over, but it was obvious to the rest of the world that Lee McNeill had failed to receive the baton within the box. Immediate protests upheld that view. The Americans had put out their reserve relay team, with dire results. The whole business made us wonder about the fairness of the judging.

In our semi were the French, Jamaicans, Italians and West Germans as the main challengers. The Canadians were there but were now a spent force with Ben languishing back in Toronto. Mac and I had had a few practice change-overs but we had run together before and, as I have said, he was one of the most experienced relay runners in the world.

We had a marvellous run. Mac came round the bend and handed me the baton and I suddenly felt an extraordinary release of pent-up energy. I just wanted to run and run to get rid of all my anger and frustration. I flew down the home straight just behind the Frenchman; we clocked 38.52 seconds for a new British record. I knew then we were definitely in with a chance of a medal, perhaps even the gold.

That all-important gold medal was still eluding the British athletes. Liz McColgan had gained a silver in the women's 10,000 metres behind the Russian Bondarenko, and Mark Rowland, in the biggest surprise of all, had won a bronze in the steeplechase. Daley had been defeated for the second year running, not by the other competitors but by the injuries that had been plaguing him. It now seemed to be down to Steve Cram and Peter Elliott in the 1500 metres and us in the relay to redeem the situation. The 4 × 400 metres team had reached the final, but without Roger Black and Derek Redmond, both badly injured, there was no way they would be challenging for medals as they had done in the past.

As the final afternoon wore on we heard that Peter Elliott had won the silver in the 1500 metres. Peter is a really gutsy runner whom I admire very much. Because of a groin injury he had had jabs of cortisone from Malcom Read before his every race, which were very painful indeed. Yet he had gone out and battled away with typical Yorkshire grit, had got fourth in the 800 metres and now, silver. It should have made the *Daily Mirror* eat their words. Crammy finished fourth to redeem himself a little.

We lined up for the final of the relay – Elliott Bunney, John Regis, Mike McFarlane and me. The gun fired and I could see how the race was progressing up until the baton reached Mac; then I had to prepare myself to receive it. I felt that we had lost a little ground on the first two legs. Then Mac took the baton. Watching it afterwards on video I saw that he ran a fantastic leg, probably the best he has ever run. Calvin and Desai Williams are the only ones to equal Mac, and neither of them was there. He brought us back in with a chance. We were fourth or fifth when I received the baton and I chased after the Russian Vitaliy Savin, who was well clear. I flew, I could feel it. I felt the fastest I have ever felt. I closed on the Russian, but not enough; we had to be content with the silver and our last chance of a gold medal had gone. My time was 8.95 seconds, the fourth fastest ever run. Not as fast, though, as old Bob Hayes back in 1964!

It was a new Commonwealth and British record of 38.28 seconds. I thought that I had, by that run, vindicated all I had believed and said down the years about where I should run in the relay. It needed someone to run that sort of speed to gain a medal; if I had run second we would not have won anything, I am convinced of that. Running on the last leg you need someone with power, speed and, above all, determination. I believe that we should have won a relay medal many more times than we have. I was pleased for Elliott, John and particularly for Mac. It was his first Olympic medal, and never was one better deserved. We went out for the ceremony and again the British cheers rang around the stadium and the flags waved. By that time all the racing was over as far as track and field went; there was only the marathon on the morrow. We had gained eight medals in the toughest Olympics ever and maintained our fourth place in the world.

I was selected, supposedly on a random basis, for my third dope test of the Olympics. It was complete chaos in Doping Control, the system seemed to have broken down completely. All the finalists were queueing and some of the relay teams, including all four Russians. The Koreans were having great difficulty in coping. The toilets were jammed with people coming and going, and it took ages to go through the procedures. I was also having a difficult time in providing a sample. I kept drinking water, but to no avail. If your mind is working against urinating, or you think about it too much, then nothing happens. Anyone who has had to give a sample at the doctor's will sympathize.

After all I had gone through I was suspicious of everything. If you took a swallow of water from a carton, left it to go outside to look at the television monitor and then returned, as I did, there is no way that you would continue drinking from that carton. You would get yourself a fresh drink. It was a legacy of the Ben Johnson affair. There was a sign beside the Coca Cola stand that said 'Do Not Drink'. If there was a problem, why was the Coke there? In fact, it became so bad that you didn't feel you should drink at all. There was suspicion everywhere, all of us wondering if there was any subterfuge going on. It is a sad, sad situation when sport reaches those depths.

The next day, in the evening, came the Closing Ceremony which I enjoyed very much. The athletes and officials all marched in together and then ran amok, running round the track with flags, forming congas and weaving in and out of the crowds. Unlike the Opening Ceremony which is always very formal, this was just the opposite, all the athletes entering the arena in one large column, not country by country. The music played, and so did we. The crowd seemed to love it. They were happy too, and proud – and so they should have been. The Koreans had done a terrific job, proved the sceptics wrong, and throughout it all they had been friendly, always smiling, nothing too much trouble.

Gradually the officials managed to contain the high spirits of the athletes and the ceremonial began. That, too, was wonderful, the best I have ever seen. As with the Opening Ceremony it was full of Korean culture and history with stunning effects. This time, though, it was laced with a touch of Spanish with dancers from the city of Barcelona, which was to be the host city in four years' time. All the spectators in the vast stands were given a Chinese lantern which lit up when two sides were put together. On an instruction all the lanterns were held up, a hundred thousand in all. It was just amazing. Afterwards came the fireworks, a huge display costing hundreds of thousands of dollars. We were just walking out of the stadium when, with an enormous bang, the display began. Our guards (we had guards with us all the time, even when we visited Itaewan) looked startled and their hands went towards the insides of their jackets but they laughed when they found it wasn't the North Koreans after all!

Safety precautions were tight even at the end. Security staff, army and police still manned the checkpoints at all the entrances to the stadium, their eyes puffed now with lack of sleep and total exhaustion. For nine days they had sat, studying and checking the accreditation cards, searching the bags, nodding us on with a smile into the interior. For nine days they had listened to the roars and cheers of the enormous crowds who were witnessing some of the greatest athletics ever performed, and they had not seen a thing.

Samaranch, the IOC President, thanked the Korean people. The mayors of Seoul and Barcelona exchanged an Olympic flag. Solemn music was played, the Olympic flag lowered, and the great flame that had shone on the proceedings for over two weeks was dimmed. It was, 'Annyong-hee kaesayeo Seoul.' Linford was on the first available flight home.

I was looking forward to flying home – we had been away almost five weeks – but I was also nervous about it. I wondered what the public reaction had been to the drug affair, wondered how the press had covered it. Would there be a hostile media reception at Heathrow?

It took us ages to go through all the checks at Seoul airport, but finally we were on the big jumbo jet that was to take us, via Tokyo and Anchorage, to Britain. On the flight Tessa Sanderson and I put together a statement that I said I would like issued by the British Board at Heathrow, giving me full support. They agreed.

We landed, the first flight in, somewhere around five-thirty. Due to its having been packed wrongly in Seoul, our luggage (everybody seemed to have a lot extra!) took more than an hour to come through to the baggage handling area. The airport manager was very helpful as we prepared to leave customs at Terminal 4 and join the outside world again. As we went through, pushing our trolleys and all keeping together in a group, a sudden burst of cheering broke out and I saw people waving Union Jacks and some calling out 'Well done, Linford!' and 'Good old Linford!' It was just a wonderful feeling and the first indication that I had of how the people at home had been so supportive, had really been concerned for me, had cared.

We pushed on through the gaggle of photographers, all snapping away. Tony kept saying, 'Keep moving, keep moving.' Then there was a rush and around me were Mum and Dad, Mandy, my sisters, nephews, cousins and lots of friends, all shouting and slapping me and obviously in great spirits. A smiling policeman stood by, and he escorted us out of the terminal. In the car park we stopped and let the photographers take pictures of us all together as a family. I felt marvellous and very happy; suddenly it all seemed worth while, even the traumas and the tears, coming home to a reception like this.

Then it was over. I climbed into a car and was driven away. The most momentous month of my life was now history.

17
Freeman of the Borough

It took me three weeks to recover from Seoul, and when I talked to most people who had been there they concurred with that time span. The Games had been a physically and emotionally draining time for everybody. It had been hot and wearing and we had been subjected to all the extra Olympic hassle – the constant security checks, both at the stadium and at the Village; the ever-present security guards; the journeying to and fro in buses; journalists and television with deadlines to meet.

It is always strange returning, re-adapting to your old way of life, re-telling the stories over and over again and answering the perennial question, 'What was it really like?' But it was good to be home, back with the family and my girlfriend, back to my Reggae music, my house and a relaxed time. I did quite a lot of sleeping. It was not, however, an entirely uneventful re-entry into the British way of life.

I was angry, when I read some of the press reports, to notice that at the time of the drug test I had suddenly become 'Jamaican-born'. The same had happened to Ben. It seemed that there was a double standard in operation. While I was winning I was British, but the slightest sign of trouble or scandal and I became something different, 'not one of us'. I did not recall, when I had won the 100 metres title in Stuttgart, that there had been any mention of my place of birth.

There was a Securicor press conference a short time after we returned from the Games, to celebrate the silver medal that we had won in the sprint relay. In answer to a question on the drug issue I said, 'Someone owes me an apology.' I did not specify whom. I didn't mention the IOC or the BOA or anybody, but I felt – feel – that for the leakages to the media that occurred in

Seoul which created the enormous pressures and hassles I had to endure, somebody owed me an apology, somebody should have had the courtesy to admit that no one ought to have had to put up with that madhouse at the Shilla Hotel. Somebody should have said, 'Sorry, Linford'.

This angered Professor Arnold Beckett, a world authority on drug abuse. Why he felt personally aggrieved I do not know, but he decided to appear on Thames Television, in an interview which was later transmitted by ITN, stating that I was a 'lucky young man' and could have lost my silver medal. He said he had gone back after the 200 metre tests to re-test my first 100 metres sample, and that he had found traces of pseudoephedrine. 'Linford Christie would be well advised to keep quiet,' he added.

I was furious. Who did this man think he was? Who had asked him to go back and test the 100 metres sample? And, of course, there would have been traces of pseudoephedrine in that sample in any case, for I had been taking ginseng over a period of months. It would be there, however, in minute amounts; so minute that even the stringent rules of the IOC were not contravened.

There was an immediate angry reaction on my behalf. Robert Watson responded publicly, condemning the remarks and saying that Beckett (who, immediately after making his statement, flew abroad for a month) had made himself ineligible for the BOA Enquiry which was being set up. Frank Dick was incensed. The BAAB, too, issued a strong supportive statement and I think there is little doubt that there was angry public feeling.

We went to Buckingham Palace and met the Princess Royal, in her capacity as President of the British Olympic Association. We had met before on the BBC's *Question of Sport* programme. She is a person I admire very much, quite my favourite sportsperson. She is understanding and she knows about sport, having competed at the highest level herself. But apart from her Olympic work – she is also a member of the International Olympic Committee – she does a tremendous job for the Save the Children Fund. Everything she does, every day, is carried out in the public eye and yet she manages, or so it seems, to keep her cool magnificently. We spoke for about twenty minutes at the

Palace and she was obviously sympathetic about the predicament in which I had found myself in Seoul.

The British Athletics Writers Association selected me as their male athlete of the year, Liz McColgan being voted female best. These awards are presented at the Park Lane Hotel in London's Piccadilly, and the evening, sadly the only social occasion that the sport seems to stage, is always very pleasant. Most everybody who is anybody in athletics seems to turn up there.

I debated with myself long and hard as to whether I should attend. The press and I, by and large, had had a tempestuous year and had exchanged a few home truths. The incidents at the Nihon holding camp and at Rome the previous year were still fresh in my memory. But in the end I felt it would have been churlish not to attend. They had done me an honour, many famous names had preceded me and it would be nice to see everybody again, to talk over the events in Seoul. So I went, and after Ken Mays, the Chairman, had presented me with the award I read them an admonitory and hopefully humorous poem. I felt better for it, anyway!

Other awards came my way, most important of which was the Thames Television Award for London's Sportsman of the Year, presented at the Café Royal by Princess Anne. I was really proud to receive the trophy, my rivals for the award including famous names, many Olympic sportsmen. And then at the turn of the year perhaps the most surprising of all was a National Opinion Poll survey to determine Britain's number one personality of the year. Prince Charles won it, with Margaret Thatcher second and John Cleese and me in third place. It was a marvellous indication to me of the tremendous goodwill and warmth that the public felt over everything that had happened in Seoul.

Steve Davis won the BBC Sportsview Personality of the Year Award, and I wish him well with that; he is the greatest ever all-round snooker player. Nevertheless I did think that perhaps in Olympic year it should have been won by an Olympian – I don't necessarily mean me, but certainly any of the gold medallists would have warranted it. Steve could have won it any year. But the most disappointing feature of the programme for me was the attention paid to Eddie Edwards, who received more exposure than anybody else. Even given that Desmond Lynam, who was co-presenting the show, was caustic in his interview, it was still wrong that a man who was such an utter failure in sporting terms should be given such publicity. If he had come fifth or sixth or even tenth in the ski jumping then maybe the fuss surrounding him would have been partly justified.

The whole business sickened a lot of people who believe in the finer aspects of sport, the competitive spirit and the camaraderie. Eddie and his total non-achievements are not, in my view, an example to hold up to any youngster. It was as if Samuel Birch, the slowest man in the 100 metres heats in Seoul, had been lauded and feted and had made a good deal of money from being so far behind everybody else. It was especially the financial aspect of the Eddie Edwards affair that galled a lot of people. He made a lot of money, money that should have gone to achievers, to men such as Wilf O'Reilly who won two gold medals in the Short Track Speed Skating demonstration events in Calgary. I find that very sad. There was a strong rumour, although no more than that, that Eddie had won the most votes in the Sportsview Personality award. I had thought it a possibility and had made up my mind that if it was the case I would stand up and leave the proceedings immediately to show my disgust and disapproval.

By this time I was training again, back on the treadmill and looking forward to an indoor season that would include the European and World Championships. Alas, it was not to be. After a marvellous Indoor Championships at Cosford I went to The Hague with high hopes of an unprecedented European Indoor double, but I sustained a foot injury that was to put paid not only to that meeting but to the rest of the indoor season as well.

We had another family Christmas, this time at my house. All my family came and my sister and I cooked the meal. It was great to be all together at the end of such a sensational and, all in all, marvellous year.

I was asked to sit for a centre-page fashion spread in the *Star*, which I enjoyed very much. A friend of mine, Ross Hemsworth, knows the *Star* photographer Lawrence Lustig very well, and they approached a shop, Jeremiah's, in Gants Hill which agreed to supply the clothes and also to give me suits and clothes for posing.

It was a good opportunity for me to show people that I am not permanently in a tracksuit. Dressing well has always been a habit with me. If I feel I am not looking smart, then I feel uneasy. It is a legacy from my younger days, the days when Mum used to make me go to meetings and airports dressed in suits and ties. She still worries. Every time I see her she wants to know if I've got a vest on – but then, I guess all mothers are the same no matter what the age of the son!

Perhaps the greatest honour, though, came in February 1989. The previous November I had received intimation that the Hammersmith and Fulham Council had unanimously voted to make me an Honorary Freeman of the Borough. It was the highest honour they could bestow upon me. A month before the ceremony in the Council Chamber the mayor held a reception and all my school-teachers came along plus a lot of schoolchildren whom I had specifically asked to be there. It was a very nostalgic few hours.

On the evening of 15 February, the night before I flew to what was to be an abortive European Indoor, the full Council gathered in the Council Chamber of Hammersmith Town Hall. They were there to approve the motion: 'That pursuant to Section 249 of the Local Government Act 1972 Mr Linford Christie be admitted as an Honorary Freeman of the London Borough of Hammersmith and Fulham in recognition of his outstanding sporting achievements, and that his name be enrolled by the Chief Executive on the Freeman's Roll.'

All the party leaders made laudatory speeches, and it was a warm feeling to have people outside my normal sphere recognizing my achievements. It somehow made those achievements all the more important to me to know that people understood the hard work that had been undergone in order to win Olympic fame. I hoped that that was the message that would go out from the ceremony.

I thought back. I had lived in the Borough for twenty-one years. I remembered that first cold, cold winter and the excruciating pain that the snow caused in my feet; remembered, too, Canberra Primary School where the little white girl had said, 'My mother said I mustn't play with blackies.' I was struck by the realization of how far I had come since then so that here I was, waiting to receive the highest honour that the Borough could bestow.

I wondered what I would have thought, as I marched in my baggy shorts and black plimsolls into the White City Stadium for that first ever race, if someone had whispered that one day

I would run in the two fastest sprint races that the world had ever seen.

I did not regret that it had taken me so long to reach the top, for I had come through at the right time. The important thing was that I had finally recognized that I had a natural talent for sprinting, and that if I dedicated myself to bringing it to full fruition then I would not have wasted my life. And this ceremony, with its formality and its history, was also a recognition of that. I will never be able to thank Ron enough for his patience in waiting.

I felt, too, that I was respected by my people, and more especially by the young black kids, perhaps the stars of tomorrow. After Seoul, often walking along the street little old black ladies would come up and say, 'We're proud of you,' and then scurry away. I cannot deny that it was nice, that I enjoyed it.

I hope that I have never pretended to be anything I am not, that I have always managed to be myself. My friends today are the same friends that I had ten or more years ago. I haven't led a blameless existence, but then nobody knows what turns life will take. When Ben's life crashed around him in Seoul, when the world was horror-struck at what he had done, I hoped I had done right by him when people asked me what I thought. I had cried for Ben, and later, in the dark night in Seoul, I had cried for myself. Perhaps all this was an accurate summary of my life: triumphs and tears.

The speeches were almost over. It was a little ironic, I suppose, that I was being honoured by the very Borough in which I and my family had suffered such heartache. In some ways it was a triumph over that harassment, proof that the spirit hadn't been broken, that Mum and Dad were there, full of pride, to see this vindication of their toil and sacrifice for their family.

The applause grew louder as I stepped forward to become a Freeman of Hammersmith and Fulham. I hoped that somehow, somewhere, Gran was aware of all this and could share the moment, part of which was rightfully hers. And then I resolved, as I accepted the honour, that we would have much more to celebrate after Barcelona in 1992.

Postscript

Throughout the early months of 1989, whilst Linford nursed a foot injury, Canadian athletics, in the aftermath of the Johnson Olympic disqualification, bared its soul at the Commission of Enquiry into Drug Abuse in Toronto chaired by Justice Dubin. It was a sad, sordid story that unfolded, about a gang of people determined upon athletics success at any price. It was a tale of subterfuge and deceit inflicted not only upon a sport but also upon the fastest man alive.

At the same time in May, the International Olympic Committee gathered in Barcelona, the home city of its President, Juan Samaranach. There were a motley collection of self-elected royalty and aristocracy and, in a distinct minority, of experienced sportsmen and women. It was at this meeting that the final, absolute vindication of Linford came, in the Analytical Results of A-Samples at the Games of the XXIVth Olympiad, Seoul, 1988. *They were represented by the IOC's Medical Commission.*

The report indicated ten positive doping cases, five from weight-lifting, two from modern pentathlon and one each from athletics, wrestling and judo. It went on:

Cases Discussed and Determined as Not Positive. Following discussion of an additional six cases reported by the laboratory as containing a substance from a banned pharmacological class, the IOC Medical Commission decided that these cases should not be considered as positive.

The words are well chosen. Certainly better chosen than those of the Medical Commission's Chairman, Prince Alexandre de Marode; certainly better chosen than those used by Professor Arnold Beckett.

Finally to win the war against drug abuse in sport the campaigners must have credibility in order to canvass public opinion and gain support and approval for their actions. To have credibility they must be consistent, not only in their words but also in their actions. There was no such consistency in Seoul. There is no consistency, amongst doctors and scientists, as to the 'allowable' levels of pharmacological substances. If the agonies endured by Linford Christie at the Seoul Olympics bring about rationalization, if no athlete suffers so again, then his torment will not have been in vain.

Appendix 1

Significant moments in Linford Christie's Career (compiled by Ian Hodge)

1978	Placed fourth in Middlesex Junior 100 metres
1979	Eliminated in heats of AAA Junior Indoor Championships 60 and 200 metres
12 May	Won Middlesex Junior 100 metres
1 July	Won Southern Counties Junior 200 metres
7 July	Second in English Schools 200 metres
8 Sept	First invitation race at Gateshead. Placed fifth in 100 metres
1980	
12 Jan	Third in Cosford Games 60 metres
26 Jan	Third in AAA Indoor Championships 200 metres
1 Feb	Great Britain debut indoors in 4 × 200 metres team against German Federal Republic
17 May	Won Middlesex Senior 100 metres
25 May	Third in Inter-Counties 100 metres
14 July	Reached semi-finals of the Olympic Trials at 100 and 200 metres
1981	
10 Jan	Won Cosford Games 60 metres
24 Jan	Won AAA Indoor Championships 200 metres, equalled record of 21.8 secs
30 Jan	First overseas international in Dortmund against Federal Republic of Germany. Set UK indoor record for 200 metres of 21.7 secs
11 Feb	Ran Invitation 60 metres at Cosford and set a personal best of 6.87 secs – his best for the next seven years
7/8 Aug	Eliminated in the heats of the AAA Championships

1982

24 July   Injured in the AAA 100 metres final when looking to place second

1983

28 May   Third in United Kingdom Championships 100 metres
18/19 June   Made Great Britain outdoor international debut against Finland in Lappeenranta, winning 100 metres and coming third in 200 metres

1984

18 May   Won Middlesex 100 metres and defeated Mike McFarlane
25 May   Sixth in United Kingdom Championships 100 metres
6 June   Fourth in Olympic Trials 100 metres
23 July   Second in AAA Championships 100 metres to Donovan Reid
18 Aug   Defeated Asquith, McFarlane, Sharp and Obeng at Crystal Palace

1985

2 March   Selected for first major championships, European Indoor, in Athens. Eliminated in the heats
25/26 May   Won United Kingdom Championships 100 metres and shared 200 metres with John Regis
13 July   Failed to finish in AAA Championships 100 metres

1986

23 Feb   Won first major international title, the European Indoor 200 metres
4 June   Set a United Kingdom record of 10.04 secs in 100 metres in Madrid
20 June   Won first AAA Championships 100 metres
27 July   Second in Commonwealth Games 100 metres to Ben Johnson
27 Aug   European champion at 100 metres in Stuttgart

1987

21 Feb   Pulled hamstring in heats of European Indoor in Lievin
27/28 June   First British athlete to win a sprint 'double' at European Cup meeting in Prague
6 July   Set a United Kingdom record of 10.03 secs in 100 metres in Budapest
30 Aug   Fourth in World Championships 100 metres in Rome

1988

5/6 March	Won European Indoor Championships 60 metres in Budapest. Also ran third in 200 metres
5/6 Aug	Won AAA Championships 100 and 200 metres, first sprint 'double' for thirty-five years
24 Sept	Silver medallist in Olympic Games 100 metres in Seoul, setting a new European record of 9.97 secs
28 Sept	Fourth in Olympic Games 200 metres, setting a new United Kingdom record of 20.09 secs

Appendix 2

Linford Christie's Year-by-year Progression

100 metres		200 metres	
1977	10.9	1977	23.2
1979	10.7	1978	22.5
1980	10.6	1980	22.0
1982	10.51	1981	21.7
1982	10.50	1981	21.6
1983	10.46	1982	21.2
1984	10.44	1984	21.0
1985	10.42	1986	20.79
1986	10.33	1986	20.51
1986	10.25	1987	20.48
1986	10.04	1988	20.46
1987	10.03	1988	20.33
1988	9.97	1988	20.09

INDEX